HOME SWEET HOME

How to Help Older Adults Live Independently

Quality Life
Resources
—————————
AAL®

Foreword

"Mom's arthritis has gotten worse and I can see it's getting more difficult for her to prepare meals. She isn't eating very well. Maybe it's time for Mom to move into a place where her meals would be prepared."

— *Mary, 60-year-old daughter*

"Dad is so unsteady on his feet. I worry about him going up and down the stairs. But he insists on sleeping upstairs because 'that's where your mom and I always slept.' I know he's fallen at least twice on those stairs. Luckily, he didn't hurt himself. But what about the next time?"

— *Bill, 53-year-old son*

"The neighbors living in the apartment next to Aunt Martha's complain that she plays her TV so loud they can hear it clearly from the far wall of their apartment. Because she doesn't hear well, she thinks the neighbors just like to complain. But we know they're right. Even the manager has warned her about this. We're afraid she may be asked to move. What can be done to help with this situation?"

— *Julia, 45-year-old niece*

The frustrations of aging. A mother wrestles with what were once routine household chores. A father is challenged by the simple consequences of living at home. Situations like these are not uncommon.

As a family member, it can be difficult to watch a loved one struggle to maintain a home and to function. You may be concerned about the person's safety and overall well-being. You may even wonder if it's time for your relative to move to another living situation.

There are times when a person may need to move from home. But for many older people, a move isn't wanted. And it isn't necessary.

The ability to function independently usually isn't an all-or-nothing proposition. Most older people who require help need it only in certain areas of their lives. Often, only a small amount of assistance is needed.

Before considering a change in living arrangements, it's important to explore alternatives to help a person be better able to function in his or her home.

In *Home Sweet Home,* you'll learn those special ways to help your loved one remain at home. You'll read about using assistive technology—devices such as walkers, zipper pulls, hearing aids and bathtub bars that promote independence. You'll learn about home modifications— simple, inexpensive adaptations such as stair railings and room conversions to accommodate a person's physical needs.

Home Sweet Home explores five areas that affect people's ability to care for themselves:

- Basic self-care.
- Meal preparation.
- Communication and mobility.
- Home maintenance and safety.
- Leisure and recreation.

You'll learn about common problems found in each of these areas—and solutions based on assistive technology and home modifications. The resource guide in the back of this booklet tells you where to go for help and how to obtain a variety of services, products and information.

Importantly, *Home Sweet Home* also provides guidance in addressing this sensitive subject of independence with your loved one, and dealing with it in a caring, helpful way.

As you read this book, keep in mind other ways to help older people remain at home. Group meal sites, home-delivered meals, and telephone reassurance and medical alert programs are available in most communities. You may also want to consider home care services or even a home-sharing plan, where another older person shares a home with an elderly relative. Your local Area Agency on Aging can help.

Home Sweet Home is for anyone who wants to ensure home for an elderly relative is a safe place, a welcome place, a place that truly can be called home.

Table of Contents

SECTION I

A Self-care
Language Primer

This section briefly introduces
you to language you may
encounter when reading about
self-care or discussing the
issue with health care
professionals.

ADLs

To be successful in getting through the day, each of us needs to deal with our surroundings. Getting out of bed and walking to the bathroom requires walking, using our eyesight and often using our sense of touch as we feel our way through the darkness. Clinically, the word used for such activity is "ambulation."

Moving someone from a bed or chair to a wheelchair, or from the wheelchair to the toilet, is referred to as a "transfer." Our ability to balance ourselves and to coordinate those movements—as well as our overall strength and endurance—all relate to our "mobility."

Using the bathroom, taking a bath or shower, and putting on our clothes are clinically referred to as "toileting," "bathing" and "dressing," respectively. Combing our hair, brushing our teeth and shaving are considered "grooming" activities.

All of these actions are known as Activities for Daily Living, or ADLs.

Being able to complete ADLs is a critical part of independent living. If there's a problem with any of these activities, there's a problem remaining independent. Possible solutions to these problems are discussed later in this book.

IADLs

In addition to ADLs, there are other activities that are part of our daily lives. Talking to one another, writing a letter, and using the telephone or the computer are issues of "communication." Driving, taking a taxi or riding a bus—getting from one place to another—are "transportation" issues.

Shopping, cooking, cleaning, taking care of our money, paying our bills, managing our medications and enjoying leisure time all play important roles in our daily lives.

These activities come under the collective clinical title of Instrumental Activities of Daily Living, or IADLs.

While IADLs are essential to our well-being, they aren't as critical in determining independent living as ADLs. Sometimes, IADL problems can be resolved simply by involving other people.

We'll also look at IADL problems—and possible solutions—in this book.

Getting the Right Start

Independent living is a tender, sometimes frustrating subject to deal with— both for you and your older loved one. In this section, we'll help you get started.

We'll look at ways to approach the topic with a loved one. What guidelines to follow in expressing your concerns. What to do when a family member refuses help. How to deal with a relative who is memory-impaired. You'll also learn about basic steps to follow in making these important decisions.

Deciding What to Do

We all want the best for our older family members. But sometimes it can be difficult to know what's best. Our ideas about "what needs to be done" may not always be the same as the views of our older relative.

Our goal should be to help our loved ones meet their needs—NOT to take over their lives. Remember, often there is no single best answer. Before making any decision, it's important to:

- Understand your relative's needs.
- Involve your relative in decisions.
- Investigate potential options.
- Recognize your relative's right to risk.

Understand your relative's needs

Before any decisions can be made about what needs to be done, you need to know what problems your loved one is facing that are making independent living more difficult. They may include:

- Meal preparation.
- Health care.
- Housekeeping.
- Financial management.
- Bathing and personal care.
- Home maintenance.
- Mobility and transportation.
- Medications.
- Loneliness.

Consider the ways your family member does manage to function. What adjustments are already being made? Then, anticipate what his or her needs will be in the future. Try answering these questions:

- What changes are being experienced by my relative? What problems and needs are these changes creating?
- Are these changes temporary? Is further decline likely?
- Is occasional or continuous help needed? How long will help be needed?
- How does my relative feel about these changes? Are they viewed as problems?
- Which, if any, of these changes are harmful to my relative or someone else?

If you have trouble determining how well your relative functions, seek professional guidance. His or her physician, nurse or social worker can help give you an objective assessment of your relative's abilities.

You may want to ask the doctor for a referral or consultation with an occupational or rehabilitation therapist. Occupational therapists specialize in identifying assistive devices, equipment and home modifications.

Keep in mind that it's hard for most people who have been self-sufficient to accept dependency. It can be a blow to an older person's self-esteem. Most older people will fight to keep their independence. Some will mask their dependency. They will insist they can manage very well, will refuse help or even attempt to control the lives of their family members.

Involve your relative in decisions

Plan with, not for, the person! No adult likes to have decisions made for him or her. No adult likes to be "told" what to do. Regardless how wise a decision might be, without involvement by the person any plan can backfire.

People generally are more willing to try an assistive device or a service—or adapt to unwanted change—when they've been involved in discussions about it.

That doesn't mean decisions are left totally up to your relative; nor should decisions burden others unnecessarily. Set limits on what you can do. Then, within those limits, your relative can make decisions.

Only when a relative has reduced mental capacity and/or there's evidence he or she is endangering the lives of others, should you question the person's ability to make decisions. For example, if your father doesn't see well and has had several minor accidents and close calls but still insists on driving, the family has a responsibility to take corrective action.

Investigate potential options

Try not to have preconceived ideas about what is best for your relative. Consider the benefits and limitations each option holds—not only from your perspective but from your relative's.

If possible, give your relative at least two options from which to choose. Your family member will feel more in control if more than one option is presented.

If it is determined that your relative cannot maintain an independent lifestyle, even with the assistance of adaptive technology, you may want to consider using community services or other housing options. For information on community services, see page 66. For other housing options, see page 87.

Recognize your relative's right to risk

You may feel changes are needed in your relative's living situation. You may have fears about what may happen. You may even tell your loved one about your concerns.

Still, you need to remember that your family member has the right to make choices—to take risks—as long as his or her mental capacities are intact and others are not endangered. Along with those rights, however, goes the responsibility to accept the consequences. It's important to make that point clear to your family member.

For example, suppose your father insists on using the stairs despite your concerns for his safety. You don't have the right to force your father to do what you feel needs to be done. But you can still communicate your concerns. You can still talk with him about your fear of him falling and injuring himself.

If your worst fear comes true and he does injure himself, you'll probably feel guilty for yielding to him. But remember, the decision was not yours—it was your father's.

Discuss consequences of whatever decisions are made. For example, one 78-year-old man insisted on climbing the stairs. Yet, when his daughter talked with him about potential consequences, it was clear that he expected her to take care of him should he fall and break a hip.

The daughter had a right to tell this to her father:

> *"Dad, I know you feel you are safe climbing the stairs. And you have the right not to make any changes. I worry about you, but I know I need to respect your decision. I've told you my fears about what could happen. You feel I could take care of you should that fear come true. No matter how much I might want to do that, chances are I wouldn't be able to because of my job and responsibilities at home. Let's talk about what else we could do if you should fall and break your hip."*

Talking About Your Concerns

The way we approach a relative about our concerns can have a tremendous impact on how receptive that person will be to what we have to say. Here are some pointers:

Know your purpose
Ask yourself the reasons you want to raise an issue with a relative.

- Do you want to discuss an issue? Or do you merely want your relative to do what you feel needs to be done?
- Are you acting out of concern or self-interest?
- Do you want your relative to make a change because it will enhance his or her independence? Or is it because it will help you worry less?
- Are there specific things different about your relative's life that warrant change? Or are you simply concerned because of your relative's age?

Identify who has "listening leverage"
Good advice is good advice, but it can make a difference who gives it. Ask yourself, who is most likely to be listened to by your relative concerning a particular issue? It may be you. It may be a close friend.

For some people, a doctor's advice is the most influential when talking about a change. For example, when asked who should talk to them about driving, many older people felt it should be the physician because, "When the doctor says you can't drive anymore, that's definite."

Good advice is good advice, but it can make a difference who gives it.

A doctor may be viewed as more objective than a family member. Being told by a doctor that a person can no longer drive because of "health reasons" will be a more acceptable reason for not driving than a relative saying, "You're no longer a good driver."

Find a low-stress time for discussion
When and where a discussion is held can have a big impact on the outcome. For example, it's best to avoid discussing emotionally sensitive issues like driving or finances when emotions are high.

In some situations, "timely moments" are good opportunities to open the door for discussion. It's also a good idea to take action during these moments of normal interaction—before a situation reaches a crisis point. For example, when Gladys saw her mother was having trouble reaching for items in the upper kitchen cupboards, she said:

> *"Mom, I see those cupboards are really high for you. I saw the neatest thing that can reach those places. How about I get you one? If you like, I can help you do some rearranging so things are easier for you to reach."*

Gladys used a positive approach. She talked about the cupboards being a "problem," rather than her mother having a problem. She also asked her mother, instead of telling her what to do.

Emphasize independence

Most of us fear being dependent. We find it hard to accept help. So, try not to emphasize your relative's dependence and what he or she cannot do. Avoid statements like, "You can't do that anymore." It often increases resistance.

Instead, try to be encouraging and supportive. For example, you might talk about how an assistive device will help your relative live better or more independently.

Take responsibility for your concerns

You're more likely to be listened to if you talk about your concerns in terms of your own feelings, rather than as though your older family member has a problem. Too often, "you" messages are given to older people. For example:

> *"Dad, you're too old to be on a ladder and painting the house. It's time you had someone else do the painting."*

> *"Mom, you keep your television too loud. You need to turn it down."*

> *"You are no longer safe on the road."*

Think about how you feel when you receive these kinds of statements from others. They tend to sound accusatory and dictatorial. People will often feel they are under attack and, as a result, will likely become defensive and put up self-protective barriers.

"I" messages tend to enhance communication. They don't put people on the defensive. With "I" messages, you speak from your own personal feelings and perceptions. You talk about the effect situations have on you. Feelings are expressed in terms of how you feel, not how the other person makes you feel.

"I" statements also tend to communicate a feeling of caring to the other person. They're hard for another person to argue about because they are your feelings and perceptions. Done correctly, they don't come across as though "I am right." For example:

> *"Dad, I really worry when I hear you are climbing the ladder and no one is around. I'm afraid you might fall and seriously hurt yourself."*

> *"Mom, I find myself getting tense and upset when the volume on the television is too high for my ears."*

"I" statements are not panaceas. If you've typically used "you" statements, that's what your family member will likely be poised to hear. As a result, your changing to the use of more positive "I" statements may not be initially heard.

"I" messages also won't be effective if they're used to manipulate another person. Used this way, problems can get worse. The purpose of "I" messages is to express honest feelings and concerns and to open the door to discussion.

"I" statements also tend to communicate a feeling of caring ...

Truly listen to your family member

Expressing your thoughts and feelings to another person is only one part of good communication. It's also important to listen and empathize—to sense and understand the emotional needs of your relative.

The worst thing to say to a person is, "You shouldn't feel ..." or "There's no reason for you to feel ..."

The feelings a person has are real. They are neither good nor bad. They just are. It's important to recognize you've heard what your relative has to say—that you understand how that person feels about a situation.

When older family members experience changes and losses, they may have feelings of fear, anger, grief, helplessness and frustration. Having someone who is willing to listen and empathize makes it easier to talk about the situation. For example, you might tell your relative:

> *"It must be difficult to have to accept help when you have always been able to do for yourself."*

Active listening is not the answer to long-term relationship problems. But it can play a role in helping to break down old barriers.

When a Family Member Refuses Help

It can be frustrating when you know your family member is having difficulty, yet refuses help. Should this happen in dealing with your loved one, try to understand the reasons behind the resistance. Ask yourself:

- Is my family member primarily concerned about cost?
- Does my relative feel he or she does not have a problem?
- Is a community service seen as welfare or charity?
- Is my family member fearful about having a stranger in the house or having possessions stolen?
- Does he or she view accepting help as a loss of control and independence? Is the person's pride a factor?
- Are the requirements for the use of a community service—financial disclosure, application process, interviews—overwhelming to my relative?

It's important to deal with your relative's feelings. For example, if your mother feels she doesn't have any problems, be as objective and specific as you can in describing your observations. Use "I" messages. Tell her you know it must be hard to experience such changes.

If your father views government-supported services as "welfare," emphasize that he has paid for the service in past years through taxes.

Introducing ideas slowly increases the chances for acceptance.

Start small

Try suggesting just one change at a time. Begin with a small one. For someone with a hearing loss, a first step could be a telephone amplifier. Later, an assessment could be made for a hearing aid and/or using a personal amplification system, through which voices or music are transmitted directly into a headset.

Introducing ideas slowly increases the chances for acceptance. The more your relative feels a sense of control in planning, the better it will be for everyone.

Suggest a trial period

Sometimes suggesting a trial period—"try it for a month"—will help. Some people are more willing to try out assistive technology or a service when they initially view it as short-term. Their attitude toward "trying it out" is likely to be more positive than when they feel "forced."

Give a gift

Some families find it works to give an assistive device, a home modification or service as a gift. It might be a Christmas gift of hair appointments for the woman who has difficulty brushing her hair because of arthritis. It could be home-delivered meals as a get-well gift after surgery. Or perhaps it's devices to make work in the kitchen easier as a birthday gift. It's best to demonstrate how the device works—then follow up to see if it's working well for the user.

Use someone familiar

Your elderly loved one may be more willing to accept help from familiar people than from a "stranger." If that's the case, think of neighbors and friends who could help.

Perhaps a neighbor could be hired to prepare a daily meal for your relative, or to clean his or her home twice a month. Is there a responsible teenager in the neighborhood who could be hired to do grocery shopping, yard work or provide transportation?

Focus on your needs

If your family member still insists that, "I'm okay, I don't need help," try focusing on your own needs rather than those of your relative. For example, say something like:

> *"I would feel better if ..."*

> *"I would feel more comfortable when I'm not here if ..."*

> *"Would you consider trying this for me so I will worry less?"*

A word of caution

Be careful about how much help you volunteer to provide. Be realistic about what you can do and tell your relative what your limits are.

For example, if you volunteer to prepare your mother's meals, do your father's laundry or clean your grandmother's house weekly, are you really willing and able to do the task for as long as the person needs it?

Sometimes, a short-term need turns out to be for several months or years. Family members can find that once they take on a task, they encounter even greater resistance from their relative when they try to hire another person or agency to do the job.

Be careful about how much help you volunteer to provide.

When Your Relative Is Memory-impaired

Only in cases such as advanced Alzheimer's disease or massive stroke are people unable to participate in decision-making. In such situations, families must take greater control in making and carrying out decisions for them.

However, you may experience anger, hostility and rejection from your older relative. This is especially true since he or she may not be able to remember discussions or agreements made. It's important to prepare yourself for "the arrows of anger" and to understand that although anger may be directed at you, these feelings are really the result of the pain of the situation.

One person said this about her difficult situation:

> *"My grandmother and I had always been close. As a result of a series of small strokes, changes occurred, which included her driving down streets in the wrong lanes. We tried talking with my grandmother about her unsafe driving, but to no avail. Finally, I had to remove her car from the premises. We talked with her about the reasons she could no longer drive and made plans for meeting her transportation needs. For weeks my grandmother was angry and accused me of stealing her car. Of course it hurt, but I also realized that my grandmother probably felt as though her car had been stolen. And because of the disease process, it was unrealistic for me to expect her to fully comprehend the true situation."*

You may find it difficult to "step in" and make decisions when a family member is memory-impaired. In fact, it can be just as hard as "stepping back" when a relative is mentally intact and making a decision you disagree with.

There may come a time when you feel your memory-impaired relative would benefit from an assistive device. Keep in mind that your relative may have a hard time learning how to use the device—or may not be able to use it at all. One daughter said:

> *"Mom had several little strokes. It affected her mental abilities. Physically, she did well until she had a major stroke in which her right leg was partially paralyzed. We thought she could benefit from a walker, but she only became frustrated trying to use it. She couldn't remember from one time to the next how the walker worked."*

The decision-making process can be a difficult one. Give yourself time and give your loved one patience and understanding.

A Model for Making Decisions

Many families find it helpful to have a plan to follow as they make decisions or solve problems. The figure depicts a six-step model.

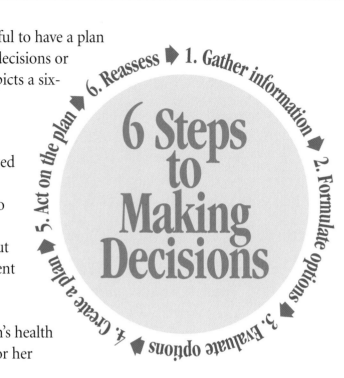

6 Steps to Making Decisions

6. Reassess ▶ 1. Gather information ▶ 2. Formulate options ▶ 3. Evaluate options ▶ 4. Create a plan ▶ 5. Act on the plan ▶

Gather information

The goal is to make an informed decision. The first step is to clearly identify the issue and to gather information. Often, families are so concerned about making a decision that pertinent questions go unasked and unanswered. A professional assessment of the older person's health and ability to function in his or her home also may be needed.

Formulate options

Once the issue has been identified, list all possible options to resolve it. Consider the resources of the older person, family and community. Health care and social service professionals can help identify options. This should be the brainstorming portion of decision-making. Keep this step separate from the actual decision step. It tends to take pressure away from people defending their positions.

Evaluate options

After all options have been identified, look at the pluses and minuses of each one. You may want to set up standards for how the options will be evaluated—criteria such as financial constraints and personal preferences. Agreeing on standards makes it easier to pick the best options. A good guideline to follow is, "Be easy on people; be tough on issues." Family members and others involved must be open and honest about their abilities to fulfill responsibilities of the options.

Create a plan

This can be the most difficult aspect of decision-making, especially if there doesn't seem to be a single best choice. At times, you may feel that there simply is no good choice and that you must select "the best of the worst." You may find that putting a plan in writing and indicating who has agreed to which tasks can reduce disagreements. A written plan can also be useful later when you re-evaluate it.

Act on the plan

A plan should not be considered as "final and forever" just because it's put into action. Situations do change. Try to establish a trial period, using the perspective of, "This seems like the best decision for now. Let's give it a try for a certain amount of time, then look at our plan again." This can be hard to do, especially if you want closure to a difficult situation. But flexibility is a key to quality decision-making.

Reassess

It's important to make plans for assessing the outcomes of the decision. Ask those involved in the decision-making process, "How well is the plan working?" Then, make adjustments as necessary.

Other Helpful Suggestions

Allow older relatives to risk

Too much loving protection can undermine an older family member's self-esteem. It's natural to want to overprotect an increasingly frail family member; however, it's usually the last thing an older person wants or needs.

The goal is to try for a balance in caring. Overestimating your relative's needs can be a problem for both of you. If you take responsibility for functions your relative can still perform—even if only with difficulty—you may make your loved one angry, depressed or more dependent.

It's more than safety

Although safety is important, it's not the only factor to consider in making a decision. Think about the type of life your older relative has lived. Consider how he or she feels about the situation. It's just as important to focus on the remaining abilities of your relative as on the limitations.

Avoid forcing your values on your relative. What one thinks is "bad" or "best" for a relative is not always true. Sometimes adult sons and daughters are concerned with a parent's "quantity of life." The parent, however, may be more concerned with "quality of life."

Avoid promises and "shoulds"

Try not to make promises like:

> *"You can always stay in your home."*

> *"We'll never put you in a care facility."*

> *"You can always live with us."*

You may not be able to live up to them. What may seem like the best solution now may not be the best five or 10 years from now when your relative's health or circumstances—or your own—change. Unfulfilled promises often result in feelings of guilt, mistrust and disappointment.

If your relative's health or living situation deteriorates, you may find yourself bombarded with "shoulds," such as:

- A caring son should invite a parent to live in his home.
- A good daughter should not allow her mother to live alone.
- A responsible child should provide care to an ailing parent.

Be careful of such "shoulds." They may come from within yourself, from other family members or from outside the family. It's important not to let the guilt of "shoulds" guide decisions.

Guilt can create all kinds of destructive outcomes: end a career, destroy one's mental or physical health, and sacrifice relationships. Guilt can reduce objectivity and reduce your ability to consider what is best for you and your family as well as your aging relative.

If a promise you are unable to keep is the source of guilt feelings, look at the conditions in which you made the promise and the current situation that confronts you. Usually, the conditions are very different. Comparing "what is" with "what was" may help you to look more objectively at the current situation. It may be easier for you to let go of a promise that is now unrealistic to keep.

SECTION III

Taking Care of the Basics

Basic self-care is an important part of independent living. Not only are the activities a critical part of day-to-day living, they also play a special role in a person's self-esteem.

This section deals with issues around bathing, toileting, personal hygiene and dressing. You'll learn what can be done to help make the bathroom and the bedroom safer places for your older loved one.

The Bathroom

Bathrooms—the "skating rinks" of the house—pose all kinds of challenges to older people. Slippery conditions can lead to injuries for people who already are unsteady on their feet. Some older people may have trouble sitting down or getting up from the toilet or the tub. Arthritis can affect their ability to manipulate doorknobs and faucet knobs.

Persons with Parkinson's disease or multiple sclerosis may have difficulty manipulating sink and tub knobs. Persons with vision or cognitive difficulties may burn themselves by turning on the hot water tap too far. If products look too much alike, such as tubes of toothpaste and muscle ointment, a person could accidentally ingest something toxic.

Fortunately, there are many items available to help make bathrooms safer. And some simple home modifications can help reduce the challenges and risks.

Doorknobs

One of the first problem areas is the simple doorknob. For someone who has restricted movement, a doorknob can be hard to manipulate—making it difficult to get in and out of the bathroom.

One solution is to wrap the knob with an adhesive tape that has a rough surface. This increases the gripping tension on the knob and reduces the need to pinch the fingers together to get a grip on the knob. While simple, over time the tape may become soiled and unsightly—not to mention a hygiene concern. Therefore, the tape should be removed and replaced at regular intervals.

Another simple solution is to change the knob to a lever. You can do this either of two ways. You can buy a rubber lever gadget that attaches to the existing knob; or, you can change the existing doorknob hardware to a levered handle.

If your relative has difficulty opening doors, all doorknobs in the house should be changed to levered handles. With levers, doors can be opened with the palm of the hand or the elbow. Levers come in a variety of designs and materials. Adaptive door levers can be found in "assistive living" product sections of your local pharmacy or supermarket. Permanent replacement hardware can be found at your local hardware store or home improvement center.

Doors

If possible, have the bathroom door open away from the bathroom. This is important for two reasons. First, if a person falls in the bathroom, he or she may be blocking the door. That makes it hard to reach the person if the door opens into the bathroom. Second, a door that opens out enlarges the entrance, making it easier to enter in a wheelchair. For easy passage through a doorway with a wheelchair, the useable width (minus hinges, door and moldings) should be 32 to 36 inches. It also offers more room in the bathroom to facilitate movement of the wheelchair. For more information on home modification, you can consult publications such as the book, *Home Planning for Your Later Years*, listed on page 80 in the resource section of this book.

If a person is wheelchair-bound, you may want to consider enlarging the door and the bathroom itself. That may seem pricey. But the changes probably will cost less than only a month or two in an assisted care or skilled nursing facility.

If you go this route, get professional help. Two videos listed in the resource section of this book can give you good pointers:

- "Changing Needs, Changing Homes: Adapting Your Home to Fit You," (see page 83).
- "Fair Housing Means Universal Design," (see page 83).

Rugs

Avoid using throw rugs in the bathroom. If a rug is needed, only use the ones with non-slip backings. You can also attach non-slip or anti-skid tape to the rug. It's a good idea to put a slip-resistant pad with suction cups on the floor next to the tub/shower.

Toilet assists

Some older persons have difficulty getting in and out of a seated position. This affects their ability to use the toilet. It also puts them in danger if they use the bathtub. They may grab onto the vanity or a towel rack to boost themselves up, neither of which is a safe approach.

There are many ways to deal with this problem. One answer is an elevated toilet seat. This product fastens onto an existing commode and requires no plumbing. Another alternative is to remount the toilet on a pedestal, although this requires plumbing, is permanent and affects all users.

If the person is unsteady, there are safety frames that attach to an existing toilet. These frames allow the person to grab onto one or both sides to help them get up and down. A more secure alternative is to install permanent grab bars. They come in a variety of shapes, sizes and components, so you can customize the installation to fit your specific needs. Because grab bars now come in many styles and colors, adding them to the home doesn't need to create an "institutional" look.

Tub bars

Probably the most dangerous place in the bathroom is the tub. As with the toilet, you don't want a person holding onto towel racks or soap bar holders for support. They're not designed to handle the weight and stress of being pulled on.

There are many styles and colors of grab bars for the bathtub and shower. They should be installed by someone who knows what to do. The mounts should be anchored into the studs of the home. Usually, the grab bar components allow for this. If you can't find grab bar components, install a backboard to the wall and studs, then attach the grab bar to the backboard. Occupational therapists and building contractors are good resources if you need help.

Other tub safety features

Much can be done to increase safety and reduce anxiety around the use of the tub. A shower mat of foam or rubber should be placed in the bathing area. Better yet, install bathtub safety treads or decorative adhesives on the tub bottom. Adhesives are safer and easier to maintain than mats. If they become soiled or ragged, they can be removed easily with an adhesive solvent

23

(available at hardware stores or home improvement centers) and replaced.

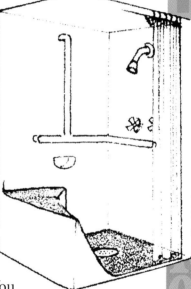

It's best to bathe in a seated position. This takes weight and stress off the legs and reduces the chance of falling. Many bath seats and shower stools are available. You might also want to consider a bath lift. This device is a chair attached to an arm which elevates the chair up and down by hydraulics. The device transfers the person in and out of the tub. Bath lifts are available at medical/hospital supply dealers. Check the telephone yellow pages. These devices can be expensive—more than $1,000—so do some research before you purchase.

Another good idea is a hand-held shower. They can be used from any position. The best ones hook to a clip or rest in a cradle that can be reached from a seated position.

If the individual is wheelchair-bound or frail, consider installing an adapted tub or shower. They come in several configurations, styles and prices. Most include features such as a seat, hand-held shower heads and scald-proof valves.

Bathing aids

To help with bathing, consider a wash or shower mitt. These mitts eliminate the problem of dropping the soap. They fit in the hand and contain a pocket for the bar of soap. The mitts come in rubber and sponge models. You can also make one out of terry cloth.

Long-handled brushes or sponges also work well. They not only help to wash the back, but reduce the need to bend to access the feet.

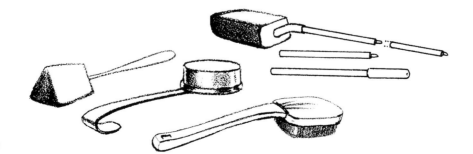

Grooming

Grooming in a standard bathroom can become a real challenge for frail and disabled older people. As with bathing, grooming should be done from a seated position as much as possible.

Basic layout

The mirror behind the vanity should be full-length to allow a person in a chair to see into the mirror. The medicine cabinet should be placed adjacent to—not behind—the vanity, so it's accessible from a seated position. The bathroom sink should be wall-mounted or of a pedestal design to allow for wheelchair or seated access.

The vanity

If the vanity is housed in a cabinet, the cabinet should be modified so the front is open. Folding doors, for example, can be installed which tuck away into the cabinet during use. This allows a wheelchair access under the sink and gives the individual easy reach to the faucet and water controls.

Even if the person is not in a wheelchair, this modification allows him or her to sit on a stool to wash, comb hair, brush teeth, etc.

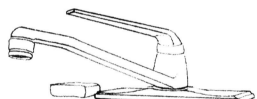

Water controls

As with doorknobs, water controls should be changed to levers. This is even more critical in the bathroom because of the added difficulty of slippery conditions. Changing the controls can be accomplished either by using "tap turner" gadgets that don't require plumbing, or by using the more permanent solution of changing the faucet to one with levered controls.

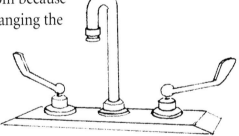

You also might want to consider various types of sensor controls that turn water on and off automatically. They've come down in price and are no more expensive than the top-of-the-line standard controls.

Adaptive gadgets can be found at the pharmacy or supermarket. Permanent hardware can be found at the hardware store or local home improvement center.

Another important addition to the sink, tub and shower is an automatic temperature and pressure control valve. Although such a device would require minor plumbing and installation, it could prevent scalding and burns. If this installation is not feasible, set the temperature on the water heater at no more than 120 degrees. This is hot enough for washing clothes and doing dishes, but not hot enough to scald.

Hand-held devices

Grooming for many disabled or frail older people is mostly a "one-handed" activity. There are many devices that can help out.

Toothbrushes are now available with built-up handles for easier gripping. For persons who wear dentures, denture brushes are available with suction bases for one-handed denture cleaning. There also are nail clippers, nail brushes and dental floss holders which can be used with one hand. There are swivel pedestals for hair dryers and adaptive holders for both regular and electric razors. Keep in mind that electric razors pose less danger of injury. You may want to consider a battery-operated razor to eliminate the risk of electrocution.

While most of us take combing our hair for granted, for others it can be quite difficult. Enlarged-grip or large-handled hairbrushes and combs are available and inexpensive. All are designed to compensate for diminished dexterity in the hand or reduced range of motion in the arm.

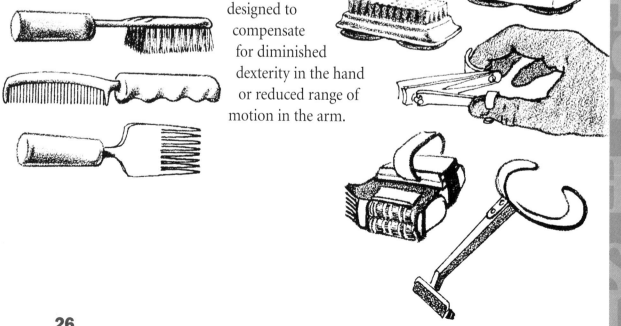

The Bedroom

For frail older people, getting out of bed can be like climbing a tall mountain. They may have to grasp the headboard to get into a seated position, hang onto the blankets to swing their legs out of bed, then lean on a night stand to help themselves up. All are potentially dangerous.

Grab bars and poles

Mounting a folding grab bar next to the bed can ease the danger. This bar mounts to the wall and folds up vertical and parallel to the wall when not in use. When needed, it swings down next to the bed providing a secure and stable grip. Another less costly adaptation is to install a vertical pole from the floor to the ceiling next to the bed.

Dressing aids

When it comes to dressing, there are several items which help reduce the need for excessive reaching or bending. Stocking aids are available to eliminate the need to bend over to put on socks, stockings or pantyhose. Dressing sticks and zipper pulls allow the user to pull on clothes and to close zippers with limited arm movement.

Adaptive clothing

For women, front-closing and pull-on bras can eliminate the need to reach behind to a back fastener. Many garments for men and women use Velcro™ for closures, which eliminates fumbling with buttons for people with limited finger dexterity. Velcro™ is readily available at fabric shops and stores that carry sewing supplies. Easy-to-use, existing clothing with which your loved one is familiar can be adapted, reducing the need to button and zip. Drawstrings or elastic sewn into waistbands also are effective means of diminishing the demands of dressing.

There are a number of devices to help fasten clothes that have buttons. Some are large-handled to compensate for diminished grip.

Other products are designed to help put shoes on. One is a long-handled shoehorn. Shoe guards allow the user to slip the foot into the shoe without bending or breaking the back of the shoe. There are also products such as a "no-tie" shoelace fastener and "elastic shoelaces" designed to eliminate the need to manipulate shoelaces.

Storage hints

Rearranging a closet can be an easy, low-cost way to make life easier. Try installing brackets in the closet so the clothes rod can be moved up or down. Hangers will be easier to reach. Store shoes and often-worn clothes at waist or chest height. Many of the new component closet units are available at hardware stores, home design and improvement centers. These units can be used to rearrange a closet at very little cost and make it much more user friendly.

Anything that can be done to reduce excessive reaching or bending and that reduces the need for delicate manual dexterity will make life easier.

The Kitchen

Food, it's been said, is our common ground. Our universal experience. The ability to prepare meals enables us to meet our nutritional needs. It can also bolster our feelings of independence and self-confidence.

However, meal preparation can also be challenging and potentially dangerous. In this section, we'll explore some of the problems and potential solutions to preparing meals and maintaining a safe kitchen environment.

Safety Matters

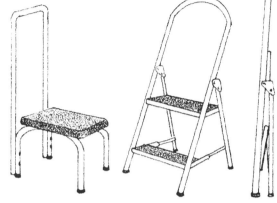

Fortunately, many changes can be made inexpensively or at no cost to make the kitchen a safer place. First among these is to rearrange items in the kitchen to provide easier access.

Every effort should be made to reduce the amount of reaching or bending a person has to do. Items on higher shelves should be moved to lower shelves. If that's not always possible, use a step stool with a handrail. The heavier the items—pots and pans or heavy containers—the closer they should be placed to the counter.

Also keep in mind that the more tasks that can be accomplished in the kitchen sitting down, the better. Meal preparation can take some time. Using a chair reduces fatigue as well as stress on the legs and feet.

Reachers

There are many different kinds of "reachers" or "reacher sticks" available to retrieve lighter items, such as bags of chips or cookies, from shelves. Reachers should never be used to retrieve heavier objects. They also should not be used to retrieve objects from overhead.

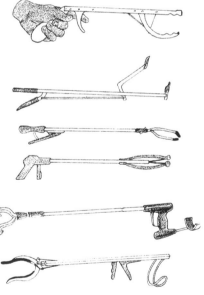

Reachers also can help reduce the need for bending to retrieve objects from lower shelves, the floor and items that fall behind furniture. Again, do not use reachers to handle heavy objects.

The better reachers have a cuff which fits under the forearm. The cuff gives the user more control and takes pressure off the wrist joint. This pistol-like operating mechanism puts the least strain on the wrist and gives maximum use of the hand and fingers.

Drawers and cabinets

Another way to bring items closer to the kitchen countertop is to add drawers under overhead cabinets. You can also install regular shelving brackets between the upper cabinets and the countertop. Shelves installed in this area can bring more items into easy reach.

A more costly alternative is to have the upper cabinets lowered on the wall or affixed to a wall bracket system which allows the cabinets to be set at different levels. You can see a demonstration of this approach in the video, "Maintaining Seniors' Independence Through Home Adaptations," produced by the Canada Mortgage and Housing Corporation (see page 83 for details).

For base cabinets, drawers are preferable to shelves. It's easier to find things in drawers. And they eliminate the need to bend over to look for things in the back of cabinet shelves.

Another alternative is standard peg-board. It can be mounted on a wall or encased in a lower cabinet on coasters, which can be pulled out to access pots and pans.

The kitchen sink

The area under the kitchen sink should be open to accommodate a wheelchair, stool or other chair. Some adjustable-height kitchen sinks are available, but if that's too radical a change, remodeling the existing cabinetry is a good alternative. This approach is demonstrated in the video, "A Home for All Ages Sampler," produced by Iowa State University (see page 83).

For better access to the sink, remove the cabinet doors and front frame. Reinforce the sides. Larger doors can be attached to the reinforced sides so the area can be closed when not in use.

A single-control extended faucet provides ease of access and one-handed use. It's a good idea to equip the sink with a spray nozzle attached to a long hose. Pots can be filled on the counter so they don't have to be lifted out of the basin.

The refrigerator

A side-by-side refrigerator/freezer has in-the-door storage the full height of the unit for both sections. That makes access easy for a person who is in a wheelchair, or who is using an adjustable stool or a secretarial-type swivel chair.

If food storage and preparation aren't big concerns, a bar-sized refrigerator installed at chair height on a cabinet with drawers could be very convenient. It will also save space and energy.

The stove

Controls for the stove or cooktop should be located at the front of the unit. This eliminates the potential for getting burned or catching clothes on fire by reaching over hot burners or pans. If the controls are not front-mounted, they should be off to the side.

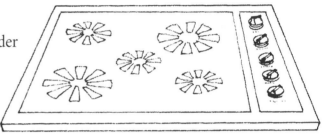

A cooktop can be installed so a wheelchair, stool or chair can fit under the counter, giving seated access to the cooking area. Some cooktops are adjustable, so they can accommodate various users.

These models are demonstrated in the video, "Why Move? Improve," produced by the American Association of Retired Persons (see page 83 for details).

Some new cooktops have ceramic surfaces that only conduct heat to a metal pot or pan. This means that even if the burner is on and you touch it, you would not get burned. Consult your local appliance retailer to see if they carry a product line which offers this feature.

If you find that your relative may be endangered by having access to the stove, make the stove inoperative. For electric ranges, flip the breaker switch or remove the fuse when not in use. For gas ranges, remove the control dials.

Consider a built-in oven with a side-opening door. Installed at counter level or slightly below, these ovens are easy to load and unload. Next best is the same type of oven with a door that folds down. Remember that while this type of door can be used as a shelf for pans, if it's hot the door can also cause burns. If you're unsure about which oven is best for your relative, you may want to check with an occupational therapist, trained nurse or contractor experienced in building/remodeling for people with disabilities.

People with reduced vision may have a hard time reading stove dials. Commercial templates are available with high-contrast, raised letters. Or, you can mark often-used settings with a high-contrast color. You can also glue a piece of toothpick to the perimeter of the dial so the user can feel for the appropriate setting. Low-vision timers are also commercially available.

The floor

Throw rugs have no place in the kitchen. They can cause falls by tripping or sliding. A textured, nonslip mat that clings to the floor would work well in front of the sink. Also, while the kitchen floor should be clean and free of grease and debris, don't wax it. Wax can make the floor slippery. It also promotes glare.

Lighting

Many times, kitchens don't have enough light by the task areas. An inexpensive solution is to install fluorescent work lights under upper cabinets. They're sold at hardware stores and home-improvement centers.

Glare can be a problem for aging eyes. Try to make sure countertops and other surfaces have a matte finish. If too much light comes through the windows during the day, a translucent shade or blinds will help to diffuse the glare. Another option is to apply a slightly opaque plastic film to the existing window panes. Check with your local glass dealer, hardware store or home improvement center.

Food Matters

Anyone who cooks knows that preparing a meal can be a real job. That task can become overwhelming for someone whose strength and dexterity are limited. Fortunately, there are lots of products to help out in the kitchen. Many are designed for use with one hand. Here are some examples.

Fruit and vegetable aids

A vegetable or fruit holder and an adapted cutting board can make food preparation much more convenient. Each is a regular carving board with two or three pins protruding from the surface. Food can be secured on the pins for slicing or chopping. The board is secured to the counter by suction cups attached to the board's base.

For peeling vegetables, use a peeler with an adapted handle. It can be steadied by hand or secured to the counter or table with a small quick-release clamp.

Specialty knives and cutters

Several specialty knives are available with various designs and handles to make the most of finger, hand, wrist and arm movement. Many can be found in gourmet cooking shops and specialty catalogues. Two examples are the rocker knife and roller or pizza cutter knife. Both are designed for one-handed use.

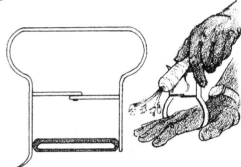

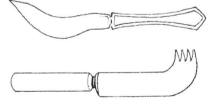

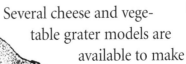

Several cheese and vegetable grater models are available to make food preparation easier. They are secured to the counter with suction

bases or clamps. Other helpful devices include a one-handed chopper, and large oven mitts.

Openers

Packaging can be difficult for anyone. Jar openers help to overcome problems. Openers that can be mounted under the cabinet can be used with one hand. They also allow really tough jars to be gripped by both hands.

Electric can openers come in hand-held and countertop models. Hand-held models are not recommended for people with severe tremors, arthritis or diminished dexterity. For these people, a countertop model would be more appropriate.

The introduction of new products or gadgets brings with it changes in behaviors. Do some follow-up! Make sure the user understands how the item works and is capable of manipulating it. You don't want the product to create more frustration or cause danger. The secret to success may simply be some emotional support and reinforcement. You may find that another form of the product is more appropriate.

Cookware

Just as there are products to help prepare food, there are also products to help in cooking it. One of the most common is a pan holder. These devices fasten to the top of the stove with suction cups and hold a pan in place to allow for one-handed stirring and to prevent spills.

Look for cookware such as saucepans with locking lids which prevent accidents on the stove and allow for one-handed operation. Try to find lightweight cookware made of materials such as stainless steel. Handles should be made of heat-resistant materials and be large enough to grasp and control the pan easily.

Other kitchen helpers include appliances with automatic shut-off features, utensils with extra-long handles such as tongs, and oven shovels to keep the cook away from hot pans and ovens.

Dinnerware

Of all the products to help maintain independence around the issue of eating, the greatest variety exists in the world of modified plates, cups and utensils. China, such as Royal Doulton, is now available with slightly recessed centers. This creates a ridge around the plate against which food can be pushed onto a fork or a spoon. The advantage of this dinnerware is that everyone at the table can use it and no one is stigmatized. Other similar dishware resembles what you would see on a picnic or in a school cafeteria.

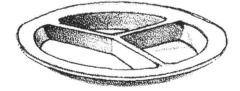

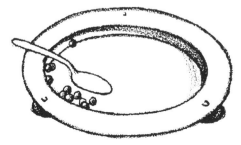

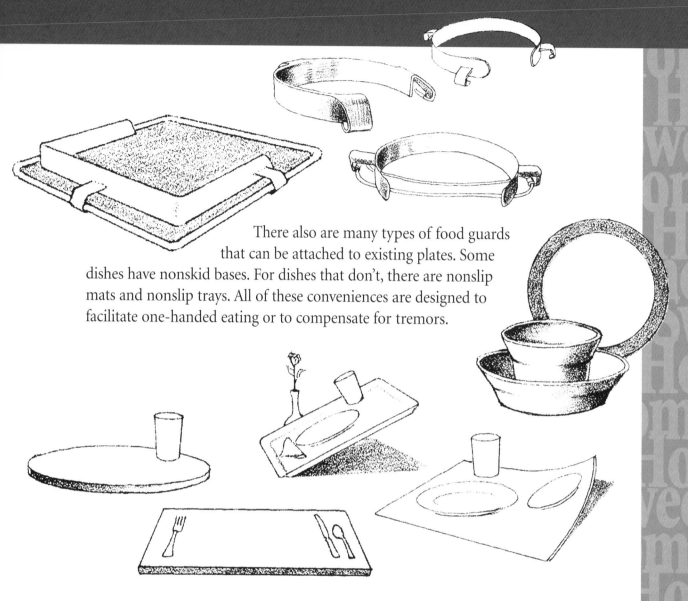

There also are many types of food guards that can be attached to existing plates. Some dishes have nonskid bases. For dishes that don't, there are nonslip mats and nonslip trays. All of these conveniences are designed to facilitate one-handed eating or to compensate for tremors.

Consider the assortment of modified cups and glasses. Some have weighted bases, double or "T" handles, pedestal bases and special insulation.

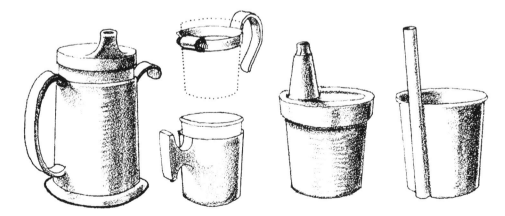

Several types of modified utensils can also be purchased. Some have large handles for comfort and improved grip. Others have weighted handles to counter the affects of tremors. Still others have extended or bent handles to make eating easier. These items are very specific to each individual's needs. It's best to shop for them with the user.

Cleaning up

Just as there are products to help prepare and cook a meal, devices are available to help clean up. You may have noticed the last time you visited a restaurant that the staff was cleaning glasses one-handed, using a brush mounted in a basin of soapy water. These devices are available for the home. While they can be used one-handed, they also free up both hands for the task.

Aesthetics are as important to older adults as to younger people. Fortunately, many specialty catalogues and stores carry dinnerware and cutlery products incorporating design principles that make them both attractive and practical.

SECTION V

Communication/
Mobility

Receiving and sending
information keeps us in touch
with the world around us—
whether it's simply reading a
newspaper, writing a
letter or talking on the
telephone. In this section, you'll
learn how to help your loved
one overcome potential obstacles
to communication.

You'll also learn ways to
help with mobility, especially
in the home.

The Printed Word

For many older people, print communication remains the traditional, the familiar and the preferred form of communication. Unfortunately, vision loss among older people is an almost universal occurrence. However, there are many products that can enhance vision. Some are small, simple and inexpensive; others are complex and can be quite costly.

Reading aids

Reading magnifiers come in all shapes and sizes. Some are small and can be handheld. Others come with their own illumination. Still others are large enough to cover an entire page at once. There are even bifocal magnifiers.

Also available are magnifiers designed to clip on to eyeglasses and others that attach to reading lamps. These products are simple, inexpensive and can help where there is a small amount of vision loss.

For someone with severe vision loss there are tabletop electronic "readers" which connect to a regular television set. Most of these readers have a reverse polarity function so that black print on white paper is reversed to a more readable white print on a black background. Portable versions of these readers are also available. Electronic readers are expensive, costing several thousand dollars each.

Writing aids

Being able to write letters and pay bills is very much a part of remaining independent. Again, there are a variety of products that can help. Bold-line writing paper helps the vision-impaired see to write. If the person has tremors, a writing guide can be used to help keep the script within a prescribed space.

Some check-printing companies offer a bold-print check line. Check your bank for availability. If gripping strength or finger dexterity is a problem, try large-handled pens and pencils. Some have a triangular or other comfortably designed shaft for easier gripping.

There are many gadgets available that attach to writing instruments. One is a simple rubber sleeve which is placed on the shaft of the pen or pencil. Another is a ball-shaped device through which the pen or pencil is inserted and secured. The user can grasp the instrument with the palm and fingers, so there's less strain on the fingers. For individuals who are experiencing hand tremors, a slightly weighted pen or pencil may prove helpful.

For people who can operate a keyboard, large-print typewriters are available. Most current computer programs provide the option of increasing the size of print appearing on the screen. In addition, there are separate computer programs designed specifically to create large print. Printouts can be in either large or regular type.

"Ergonomics" is an important concept today. It simply means making adjustments in items to fit the abilities and comfort of the person who uses them. Many products, from automobiles to writing pens, are ergonomically designed. This quality makes them easier to use by everyone, especially individuals who are experiencing changes in their physical and sensory abilities.

The Telephone

Just like the rest of the population, older people rely primarily on the telephone to stay in touch. There are many different telephone-oriented products designed to compensate for vision, hearing and cognitive deficits. They range from the simple and inexpensive to the complex and costly.

Vision aids

If the home still has rotary dial telephones, the numbers may be hard to see. A large-print template can help. It has large black letters on a white background and attaches to a standard desktop rotary phone. If the home is equipped with standard touch-tone phones, a different adapter is available. This lightweight plastic converter attaches over the existing pushbuttons. It has large buttons with easy-to-read numbers. Some versions of this adapter have textured surfaces to help identify the numbers. Both of these adapters are inexpensive.

Another alternative is to buy a new phone that has large, easy-to-read buttons. They come in a variety of designer models, many with high-contrast lettering. These phones are available in telephone, discount catalogue and some department stores.

Hearing aids

There are a number of products available to help people with hearing loss use the phone more effectively. Some of these products attach to the phone; others are built into the phone itself.

If you're buying a new phone, check to see that it has an adjustable volume control. If you don't wish to change phones, consider the many different adapters that will accomplish the same objective. Some attach directly to the telephone and are compatible with a hearing aid. Another less-expensive version attaches between the phone and the receiver.

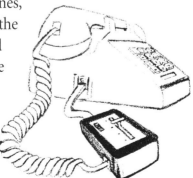

Portable, pocket-sized amplifiers are also available. They are battery-powered, and simply clip onto the receiver of any standard telephone.

Sometimes, just hearing the telephone ring can be a problem. A solution is a signal converter. This device converts the ring of the telephone to a sound more easily heard by persons with hearing impairments. Another version of this device changes the bell sound to a flashing light signal. Some use standard lighting; others use an intense strobe capable of waking a sleeping person.

For persons with severe hearing loss, you might want to consider acquiring a TDD (telephone device for the deaf). Information on these products should be available from your local telephone company. Or, consult one of the resources listed in the resource guide which is included in this book, beginning on page 62.

Cognitive aids

To help with memory and judgement difficulties, many phones have features such as memory or programmable redial. Auxiliary devices are also available for standard phones, but their cost is no less than the new phones with these features.

There are several ways to make memory redial easier to use. Family or friends can program the phone for the end-user and explain how automatic redialing works.

For phones with memory redial by number, try printing a simple listing next to the phone with corresponding numbers. For example, "son" may be the number 1, "daughter" may be number 2, and "pastor" may be number 3.

You can also include photos next to the list. For example, next to the picture of the son is a number 1, next to the daughter's photo is number 2, and so forth. Telephones such as the Teleface™ photophone have incorporated these ideas and are now commercially available. Check specialty catalogues and stores.

Grasping aids

For persons needing help grasping the phone, hand-clip phone receivers are available. These U-shaped frames help the user to hook the receiver to the palm of the hand. Another solution is a shoulder rest which attaches to the receiver. This device also frees up the hands during a conversation. It can be found in phone, department, drug and office supply stores.

Another excellent solution is the speaker phone. This feature is common on many of today's phone models. It allows for long, stress-free conversations. Auxiliary units are available for both regular reception or with amplifiers for the hearing impaired.

Augmenting devices

Sometimes following a stroke, the ability to speak can be severely impaired. Speech aids are available, including those with hard-copy printouts and others that produce human-quality speech. An assessment should be made by a speech-language therapist, who will be aware of what is currently available. For more information, contact the American Speech-Language-Hearing Association (see page 75 for more information).

For some of the products featured in this chapter, you may wish to seek professional assistance. Occupational therapists and others can help determine the most appropriate products and tell you where to obtain them. A listing of professionals begins on page 63 of this book.

Mobility

Equally important to staying in touch is the ability of older persons to get around in their home and community. Several aids are available to help people remain mobile so they can continue to live independently.

Canes and walkers

While canes are a common aid, most are too high for their users. A cane that isn't properly fitted can throw people off balance and make them less stable on their feet. The height of the cane should be determined by a physical or occupational therapist. A home health aide or visiting nurse may also be able to help.

In addition to height, other factors should be considered, including the handle. The most common cane handle is the U-shaped neck. This type of cane can be hard to grasp. Ball and T-shaped cane handles can be easier to hold for people with limited finger strength or severe arthritis.

The cane tip should be a suction type and kept in good repair for traction and to prevent slippage and/or scratching of floors.

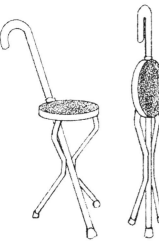

The features of a cane should be based on the overall health status of the user. For example, adding a forearm cuff to the cane can help people who need to reduce wrist and hand strain. Quad-style canes (those with four legs mounted to the base of the cane shaft) are more stable and secure, but also add weight. That can put a lot of stress on older people who have reduced upper body strength.

Standing and walking can be very fatiguing. For walking outdoors or any distance, a cane with an attached seat may be especially helpful.

Canes support about 20 percent of body weight. If more support is needed or if balance is a problem, a walker may be a better choice. Walkers support about 50 percent of body weight and are more stable than canes.

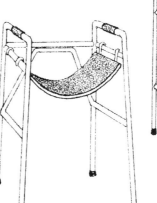

There are a variety of accessories available for walkers. Canvas bag attachments let users carry books, refreshments—even cordless phones—with them as they move about the house. Choose accessories carefully. If used improperly, such as putting too many items in the canvas bag, they can be hazardous.

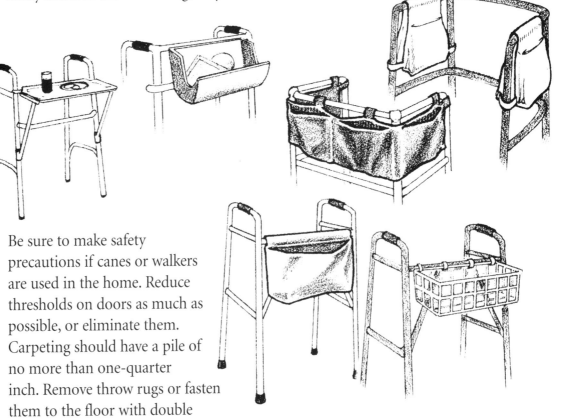

Be sure to make safety precautions if canes or walkers are used in the home. Reduce thresholds on doors as much as possible, or eliminate them. Carpeting should have a pile of no more than one-quarter inch. Remove throw rugs or fasten them to the floor with double adhesive tape. Secure all electrical cords at the base of walls or behind furniture to avoid the potential for tripping. Don't use canes on stairs unless the stairs have both a banister and a wall-mounted handrail.

For more information on these safety issues, you may want to refer to the video, "A Home for All Ages Sampler," produced by Iowa State University. It's listed on page 83.

Stairs and ramps

Stairs can impede mobility. One way to solve this problem is by installing a stair lift or a home elevator. Both are substantial investments. But keep in mind that they are not nearly as costly as moving to an assisted living facility.

If the home has outside stairs leading to the entrance, railings should be on both sides of the stairs and around any landing.

Ramps can be less demanding than stairs for walking and they are essential for wheelchair access. Ramps should have railings on both sides. Portable ramps are commercially available. Wooden ramps can also be built over existing stairs. It's best to contact a knowledgeable contractor before building—and be sure to check out local building codes. For the "do-it-yourselfer," contact your State Assistive Technology Project (see page 74, "Assistive technology projects") for technical and construction information.

Single-level living

Another option to help with mobility is to create the living environment all on one level. This usually means using space on the main floor and moving an upstairs bedroom to the lower level. Depending on the size and features of the main floor bathroom, some remodeling may be required.

You may also want to consider making at least one entrance on the main floor wheelchair accessible. These issues are explored in several videos listed in the resource guide, including, "Why Move? Improve" (see page 83 for details).

Furniture adjustments

Often, the simple acts of sitting and standing can be difficult for an older person. Raising the height of furniture such as chairs, sofas and beds can make these activities easier. Chair-leg extenders work well and can be purchased commercially. Wooden studs also can be cut to fit under the bed frame, cradling the legs and raising the bed.

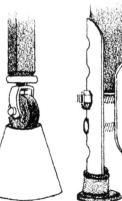

Many styles of chairs can be purchased that help a person sit and stand up. Some use a "rocking" principle; others are electrically powered and help the occupant reach a standing position. Another portable version works on a spring-loaded mechanism.

Transportation

The subject of transportation is a complex one, especially when dealing with the deeply personal topic of driving. There are many publications and resources available that address this subject. Therefore, the issue is not covered in this section. However, it's important to keep in mind that an older person's decision whether to drive should be made in consultation with a physician and the family.

Also know that under the Americans with Disabilities Act, public transportation must be wheelchair accessible. Call your local transit authority for more information.

Often, transportation services are provided by the local Area Agency on Aging. Some communities provide transportation services through local senior centers and churches. Call your local Area Agency on Aging's Information and Referral Service for more information (see page 74 for details).

Taking Care: Safety at Home

One of the major concerns associated with a frail person is home safety. Fortunately, there are products and strategies that can help make the home a safe, comfortable place.

In this section, you'll learn about many of those important ways to help your loved one— from simple housekeeping ideas, to various home maintenance suggestions.

Room Safety and Comfort

Three rooms need the most attention when you are helping an older person live comfortably and safely at home: the bathroom, the bedroom and the kitchen. Here are some safety tips for each room.

The bathroom

Remove glassware from the bathroom. Use plastic, break-resistant cups and tumblers. Install water-heat and pressure monitors on the sink and tub/shower to protect against burns and scalding and to control pressure. Set the water heater no higher than 120 degrees. If another person lives in the home, ask the occupant not to use the water while the older person is grooming or bathing.

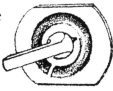

Use night-lights between the bedroom and the bathroom. They can be regular night-lights or those activated by motion sensors.

Many older persons are on more than one medication. Often, these medications are taken at different times of the day. There are a variety of pill organizers on the market that can help.

A family or friend can fill the organizer, so the individual can retrieve the pills when needed. Organizers usually must be filled weekly. Take care when selecting the organizers. Some can be hard to open.

There also are products to help older people who must take liquid medications. Liquid drug medication guides accurately measure the required dosage. A syringe magnifier and syringe needle guide can assist in measuring the accurate dosage and filling the syringe without injury.

A number of different "talking" weight scales are available to help the vision-impaired. These scales also eliminate the need to bend over to read the scale.

The bedroom

Bed lamps play an important role in the safety and security of older people. All too often, however, the on-off knobs on lamps can be small and hard to turn. Fortunately, there are several products that can help. A lamp-switch extension device can be fastened to an existing knob, making it larger and easier to grasp and turn.

An even easier solution is to install a "touch" adapter. This device turns a lamp on and off by simply touching any metal portion of the lamp. These devices also come in designer controls, which sit next to the lamp. Check with your local hardware or lighting store.

Another alternative is a sound-activated light switch that works by a clap of the hand. This can also be handy for turning on and off the TV or radio without having to get out of bed.

Hardware stores also have timing switches programmed to provide illumination in the morning when the individual gets up. This device also eliminates the worry of forgetting to turn the light out at night. It's also effective for people with cognitive impairment.

A more complex environmental control unit allows the person to turn on lights, appliances, even unlock the front door or summon help from a chair or bed without getting up.

Many clocks are available that alert the user through synthetic speech, vibrations and/or a flashing alarm. These products can be programmed not only to wake a person in the morning, but also to remind him or her to take medication, watch a favorite TV program, call family or friends, or eat a meal.

The kitchen

Install a fire extinguisher in the kitchen. It should be small, lightweight, easy to use and capable of putting out a grease fire. The older person should be thoroughly trained in how to use the device to avoid a panic situation in case of fire.

Install smoke detectors in the home. They should be the type where the batteries can be checked with a flashlight. This eliminates the need to climb up on a ladder. For the vision or hearing impaired, fire alert systems are available that use a blinking strobe light or vibrations to alert the occupant to danger.

A water-heat and pressure valve should be installed to prevent burns and scalding. Set the water heater at no more than 120 degrees. This is still hot enough to do dishes and laundry but not hot enough to burn.

In addition to consulting professionals, check the services provided by your local telephone company and electrical/gas utilities. They may have products and services to assist you. For more information, see the Professional Resources list which begins on page 75 of this book.

Other Home Safety Tips

It's important to eliminate clutter from living areas. Remove excess furniture such as coffee tables. Install protective corner pads on furniture with sharp edges. Try to reduce the amount of knickknacks. Cleaning them can be exhausting. Following are other safety and comfort suggestions for the home.

Stairs

Sufficient lighting in stairwells is critical. On-off switches should be at both the top and bottom of stairs. Railings should be on both sides of the stairs and extend beyond the actual steps. If stairs are carpeted, the pile should be tight and no longer than one-quarter inch. The carpet should be tightly secured to the treads of the stairs. For the vision-impaired, phosphorescent or other high-contrast tape can mark the leading edge of each step. Remove throw rugs from around the top and bottom of the steps.

Entrances

Entrances should be well-lighted. Consider motion sensors. They provide light without having to fumble with a switch. A task light next to the keyhole can make opening the door easier.

There are a variety of door operators that also make opening the door easier. Some don't require the use of hands. Entrance doors should have catches, so they remain open for someone using a wheelchair or a cane, or who is carrying packages.

Housekeeping

Several products are available to help with this important area of independent living. Long-reach cleaning brushes, dustpans, brooms and sponges reduce reaching and bending. A foot mop can cut the need to kneel or bend over. To avoid carrying heavy buckets of water, use an indoor hose. Containers can be filled outside of the sink or tub, and a bucket stand can move the container without having to carry it. Try other ways to make the home easier to maintain. For example, safety treads in the tub are easier to clean than mats.

Summoning help

Accidents often happen when an older person hurries to reach a ringing telephone. After an accident, it may be difficult to reach the phone. Therefore, there should be at least one phone on each floor of a home. Locate the phones where they can be reached from a sitting or prone position—and where the person spends the greatest amount of time. A cordless phone is a good idea. It can be carried, so there's no "running" to catch it before it stops ringing, and no cords to trip over.

For persons with disabilities or who are very frail, an emergency alert/ response system might be appropriate. They come in many models and price ranges. Some call pre-programmed numbers. Others are wired directly into 24-hour-a-day monitoring services.

SECTION VII

Leisure and Recreation

Leisure and recreational activities play a major role in the lives of older people. How much they can continue to participate in their favorite activities can have a tremendous impact on their overall well-being.

This section includes a sampling of the wide range of products that can help people continue to enjoy themselves, despite physical or sensory challenges.

Reading helpers

There are a variety of book holders on the market that can help someone with a weak grip, severe arthritis or tremors. The holders allow for reading while seated or lying down. There also are devices to help with page turning. They attach to the palm of the hand with a U-shaped clamp. Along with a wide range of magnifiers, large-print books are available. Also popular are books on tape; many times, current best-sellers are on tape and can be purchased.

FULL PAGE MAGNIFIER
This item will enlarge an entire page of print.
...not to be that is the question.
...nobler in the mind to suffer the...
...arrows of outrageous fortune...
...take arms against a sea of troubles...
...by opposing end them

TV adapters

People with hearing deficits can benefit from a telecaption adapter. This device connects to any television and converts programs that have been "closed-captioned" for the hearing impaired. Words appear as white letters on a black background. Most new sets have this capacity built into the television. Check with your local electronics dealer. Also, check to see if the adapter has an outlet for earphones. Earphones can help by blocking out noise in the room.

Earphones with separate volume controls also allow an individual to listen to the TV at a much higher level than that of others in the room. In some areas, DVS or "descriptive video service" is available for the visually impaired. Check with your local television stations or cable service.

Playing cards/games

Low-vision playing cards are available for persons with eyesight problems. The cards come in a variety of styles with large numbers and markings. Other handy devices include card holders and card shufflers. The shufflers are tabletop devices that shuffle up to three decks of cards at a time. They come in either hand or battery-powered models.

For those who enjoy chess, there are oversized chess sets. Some toy stores also have large-print board games.

Leisure and recreation are not often thought of as critical to maintaining an individual's independence. However, their contribution to the quality of life may provide the emotional support needed for that individual to want to remain independent.

Sewing aids

Hand-held sewing machines and electric scissors can compensate for reduced finger dexterity. There also are several different styles of needle and yarn threaders commercially available. Knitting and embroidery can be done one-handed with devices designed to clamp onto a table.

Gardening help

Look for garden knee pads and mats that protect and cushion the knees. Long-handled sprayers—some with adaptive handles for easier grasping and control—can help with watering. For raking, seeding, tilling and pruning, there are many types of long-handled garden tools and adaptive handles. They eliminate the need to bend or reach and reduce the risk of falls. Choose hand garden tools with larger handles and nonslip surfaces for easier grasping and control. Some are specially weighted to make garden work less tiring. You may want to consider a terraced garden so that gardening can be done from a seated position.

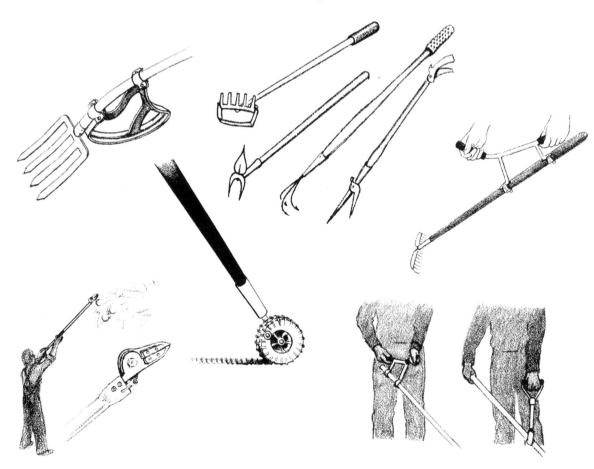

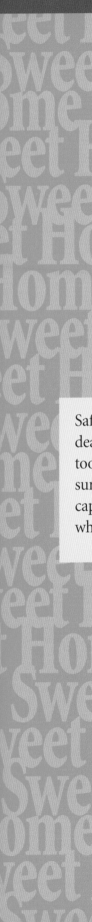

Repair work helpers

To help with repairs around the house, your local hardware store has tools such as saw guides, T-squares and levels. Liquid plastic or putty can enlarge handles to make tools easier to grip. You can also use gripper tape. Raised-line markers can be applied to tools and other surfaces to make them three-dimensional. A large-print labeler can make supplies easier to find.

Safety, especially when dealing with adapted tools, is critical. Make sure the individual is capable and comfortable when using them.

SECTION VIII

Resource Guide

Knowing help is needed is one thing. Knowing where to find it is quite another. This section offers you a good start. It lists resources that provide services, products and information to make living at home easier and less dangerous for your loved one. There is information on other housing options, too.

Keep in mind that this listing is an overview of many different types of resources. AAL has no firsthand knowledge of any specific resource listed here. You'll need to find what's available in your own community and use your own judgment about resources that may work for you.

Professionals

There are many specialists who can help older people and their families with decisions about using assistive devices and making modifications in the home. The following sample of professionals is listed in the order that may be the most useful to you and your relative living at home.

Occupational therapist

The name is somewhat misleading. Occupational therapists work with people of all ages. They are trained to help others make the most of their abilities, including the ability to live independently. They evaluate how well people function, recommend products to help, and train people how to use the products. They can also recommend modifications to the home. Many work with contractors, customizing home modifications to meet the needs of their clients.

When public or private reimbursement is involved, the occupational therapist may collaborate with a physical therapist or physician. Where speech or hearing is a concern, collaboration may be with a speech-language therapist or an audiologist.

Occupational therapists have various guides and checklists to help determine how well a person functions at home and what, if any, modifications are needed. You may want to ask if any of these checklists are available for you to use.

Some occupational therapists are in private practice and are listed under "Health" or "Home Health Services" in the yellow pages. You can also call your local hospital and ask the physical/occupational therapy department for a referral. Another option is to contact local nursing homes for occupational therapists who work with their residents. If you need more help, contact the American Occupational Therapy Association (AOTA) listed under Professional Resources in this section (see page 75).

Home health nurse or visiting nurse

Home health nurses are either in private practice or work for home health service companies. Look in the yellow pages under "Health Services." You may also contact your local hospital or nursing home to see if they might recommend nurses under contract who also do home-based work. Ask whether the nurse has had training in geriatrics or rehabilitation medicine. Nurses who haven't had such training may not be as aware of assistive devices. Instead, they may rely on human interventions to solve problems.

Physical therapist

These specialists are trained in how to strengthen muscles and retrain them to function after severe trauma such as a fall, accident or stroke. Their help is critical with problems that involve walking. Consult them on issues concerning use of a cane, wheelchair or walker.

Some physical therapists are in private practice and can be found in the yellow pages under "Physical Therapists." You can also contact local hospitals or nursing homes for referrals. If you need more help, contact the American Physical Therapy Association (APTA) listed under Professional Resources in this section.

Physician

Family doctors play an important role in determining the potential effectiveness of interventions. This is because they can diagnose many related factors that may influence how successful changes in the home will be. However, unless they specialize, many general practitioners don't receive much training in geriatrics or rehabilitation medicine.

For third-party payment, public or private insurance, physicians must "prescribe" the products as a medical necessity. Consult your physician and ask if his/her training has included geriatrics or rehabilitation medicine. If the training has been minimal, ask for a referral.

Before you meet with your doctor, you may want to write for a copy of the publication, *Primary Care for Persons with Disabilities: Access to Assistive Technology,* published by the American Medical Association (see page 81 for details).

Geriatrician

A geriatrician is a medical doctor who has received specialized training in the physiology and pathology of the aging body. These physicians are more acutely aware of the effect of drugs and drug interactions in an older person. They are more likely to make a correct diagnosis when dealing with older adults than are physicians who have not had this training. Most also have at least some training in the psychology of older persons. Not all geriatricians receive training in rehabilitation medicine or are aware of purely non-medical alternatives (assistive living products). Therefore, if you feel these alternatives may be appropriate in your situation, ask your geriatrician for a referral to another physician. In most cases, the additional services of an occupational or physical therapist may be all that is required.

Social worker

A social worker can be a big help to the family when a relative is trying to adjust to challenges that come with aging. Here is a "neutral" third party who can help everyone come to terms with whatever the situation is.

A social worker not only provides counseling, but also has a network of resources that can help with everything from funding sources to care/case management (professional management of the individual's health and/or financial concerns). You can locate a professional in case management by calling your local Area Agency on Aging.

Care manager

A care manager is an individual who provides professional "management" of an individual's health and/or financial concerns. This can occur in an institutional setting or in the community. Most care managers, but not all, have social work training. Their job is to marshall existing resources and manage them to respond to the needs of their clients. If you think a care manager would be helpful, contact the local Area Agency on Aging or find a local care manager through the Internet at **www.caremanager.org**. Hospitals may be another resource. Some care managers have private practices.

Gerontologist

Gerontology is a broad professional field that is concerned with the social aspects of the process of aging. Most gerontologists have had some training in the physiological, psychological and pathological changes associated with growing older. Some professionals hold degrees or certificates in gerontology and then specialize in social work, medicine, research, teaching, public policy, agency management, etc. Other professionals hold degrees in the specific areas in which they work, but their work is exclusively with or on behalf of older adults.

Other professionals

Other professionals may be needed, ranging from a podiatrist to a psychologist. Any of the above-listed professionals should be able to help you determine who needs to be involved and how to contact them.

Community-based Programs

There are many community-based services that can help older people live independently in their homes. Most people who require help need it in only certain areas of their lives, and sometimes only for a limited time, for example following surgery or during recuperation from an illness. If they receive such assistance, they can continue to remain in their homes. Occasional help (with grocery shopping, transportation, heavy housecleaning, yard maintenance, caregiving to a spouse and other specific tasks) from family, friends, neighbors or community agencies is sometimes all that is needed. Also, some community programs may simply enable a person to enjoy life more, and that, too, is important.

Older people comment about the benefits they received from using community programs:

> *After my spouse died, I just didn't feel like cooking for myself. I started going to the senior center for lunch. It was good for me. I got out of the house, ate one good meal a day and started going on the senior center's weekly day trips.*

> *My hands and legs are painful and badly crippled from arthritis. Eventually, I could no longer do the yard work, vacuuming and other household tasks, but otherwise I was able to care for myself. Although I now live in an assisted living facility, I was able to live in my beautiful home 10 years longer because of the help I got with these chores.*

> *After I returned home from the hospital, I needed a lot of help. The one thing I didn't want my son to do was help me to bathe. Having the home health aide in my home twice a week made bathing easier and less embarrassing.*

Services vary from community to community. A wide variety of services are available to older people who live in urban and suburban areas, while in small towns and rural areas, community services are more limited.

To find out more information on the services available in your community, a good place to start is the state or local Area Agency on Aging (AAA), (see page 74). This agency specializes in locating, coordinating, and at times, directly providing services. The Eldercare Locator, financed by the U.S. Administration on Aging, also can provide information about services in your area. Call (800) 677-1116, Monday through Friday, 9 a.m. to 8 p.m. (EST), or visit **www.aoa.dhhs.gov.** on the Internet. Many social service agencies, home health agencies and senior centers can also help you locate services, or may even provide the needed services.

The following are examples of community-based programs that can help address specific concerns.

Concern	Program
Meal preparation or obtaining food	

Congregate meals
Meals are provided in a group setting, often located in senior centers, schools, churches and housing projects for older adults. Social contact and activities are emphasized, as well as providing nutritious meals. Transportation is sometimes provided. Participants contribute what they can to the cost of the meal.

Home-delivered meals/Meals on Wheels
Meals are delivered daily or several times a week to homebound persons who cannot prepare their own meals.

Food stamps
Low-income people who qualify for Supplemental Security Income or Medicaid may be eligible for financial support through food stamps, which can be used at grocery stores participating in the food stamp program.

Grocery delivery
Some grocery stores will deliver groceries to an older person's home for a small fee. In some communities, groceries can now be ordered over the Internet from **www.HomeGrocer.com, www.peapod.com** and a growing number of local grocery stores with Web sites.

Household tasks	**Homemaker services** Assistance is given with daily living needs, such as grocery shopping, cooking, light housekeeping (e.g., vacuuming, dishwashing, changing linens and laundry), and errands. Some homemakers may provide some personal care. Homemakers do not provide health care and nursing services.
Home repairs	**Handyman and chore service** Workers are provided at reduced cost for minor home repairs, home maintenance (e.g., putting up storm windows, mowing the lawn), heavy household cleaning, and other chores. The service usually does not include major home improvements. **Home improvement/weatherization** Limited home improvement grants or loans are available to older people who meet income eligibility guidelines. Funds can be used for roofing, making ramps, and insulating a home.
Transportation	**Senior transportation** Frequently listed in the telephone directory under names such as "Dial A Ride," transportation may be available for specific reasons such as medical appointments and treatments, grocery shopping, nutrition site programs, and other necessary travel. Some programs have buses or vans equipped with lifts or ramps for wheelchairs. **Volunteer drivers** A service may be provided by volunteers who use their private vehicles to transport elders to and from their destination. **Taxi service** Some communities offer discounted taxi fares or vouchers for older people.

Loneliness	**Telephone reassurance** Telephone reassurance programs provide daily or regular telephone contact with homebound or at-risk older people. The older person calls in or a telephone call is made to him or her at a pre-arranged time. If the telephone is not answered, the caller immediately notifies a designated person or agency (friend, neighbor, police or fire department) who investigates. **Friendly visitors/Senior companions** Either volunteers or paid individuals provide social contact, often once or twice a week, for older people who are homebound or living alone. They do whatever a friend might do: offer friendship and conversation; write letters, read aloud, or just sit and listen; assist the person with his or her interests or hobbies; or take the person on walks or other outings.
Emergency alert	**In-home medical alert program (also known as a personal emergency response system or "lifeline")** An electronic device, usually worn by the older person, sends a signal to a central dispatcher, often located at a hospital, if he or she falls or needs help. Emergency assistance is summoned if the person does not answer the telephone. Help is available round-the-clock. **Community alert programs** In some communities, letter carriers, newspaper deliverers, utility meter readers, and other people who have contact with the older people in the course of their jobs, are trained to recognize those who may need help. Where the postal alert program operates, the postal service contacts a designated person when mail is accumulating in the mailbox of an older person.

Activities	**Senior center**
	Most senior centers offer a variety of recreational and social activities. They also serve as clearinghouses for information. Some also provide a range of supportive services—information and referral, meal programs, financial counseling, in-home services, legal assistance, health screenings, grocery delivery, help in applying for Medicare and Medicaid, and transportation.

Bookmobiles/Library

Local libraries often offer special programs and services for older people.

Home health care	**Home health care agencies**
	Medical care can be brought into the home, even for people who are seriously ill or dying. Home health care agencies, both public and private, offer a range of services, from assessing a person's needs to providing the needed care. Services generally include skilled nursing care; physical, occupational, and speech therapy; social work services; and personal care—assistance with bathing, dressing, grooming and exercising.

Some home health care is reimbursable by Medicare, Medicaid and some private health insurance policies, but only under very specific conditions.

Personal care	**Home health aides**
	Home health aides, often employed by home health agencies, provide nonmedical services to assist older persons in their homes. They may assist with a variety of activities, including bathing, dressing, grooming, meal preparation, and reminding and supervising the taking of medications. These workers are also called personal care aides, personal care assistants, nurse's aides or nurse's assistants. *Certified* home health aides have successfully completed a state-required training program.

Personal care
(*continued*)

Parish nurses

Complementing the ministry of pastors, deaconesses, deacons and other church workers, parish nurses combine religious faith with caregiving. Parish nurses are affiliated with several denominations in the United States and around the world. They usually are registered nurses. However, their ministry does not typically involve performing hands-on medical procedures. Instead, parish nurses most often provide health education, health counseling, referral to community resources and spiritual support. They may monitor clients' use of medications and inquire about the adequacy of their diet. In times of special need, parish nurses may coordinate caregiving volunteers and arrange for church members to cook meals or provide transportation to medical appointments.

Support for caregivers

Adult day services

This program—also called adult day care or adult day health care—is for frail older people who need assistance, but not continuous care. The program is available usually on a weekday or hourly basis. Services range from social and recreational activities to health care (therapy, assistance with medicine, and personal care). Transportation is sometimes provided. This program is particularly helpful for the caregiver who works during the day or needs a break from caregiving.

Respite care

Respite care services—which may be provided in the home, out of home in a group setting, or overnight and for an extended time in a care facility—give families temporary relief from caregiving. In the home, respite providers offer companionship, activities and light assistance to the person. They do not provide hands-on care, but they will assist the person to the bathroom when needed.

Support for caregivers (*continued*)	**Caregiver support groups**
	These groups provide family caregivers with the opportunity to talk and share with others who have similar experiences and problems. Groups have formed in many communities for families providing caregiving to relatives who have specific medical conditions such as cancer, stroke, Parkinson's disease, or Alzheimer's disease and other kinds of dementia.
End-of-life care	**Hospices**
	A hospice program offers a range of care and support services to terminally ill patients and their families during the end-stage of disease. Hospices typically offer: medical, nursing, homemaker and home health services; respite care; and counseling and bereavement services.

Costs for the above services vary depending on the type and extent of service provided. Some programs charge on a sliding scale, and the fee is determined by the ability of the person to pay. Others have a set fee based on the services provided and hours of staff time required. Some volunteer groups provide services at no charge or for a small donation.

Products and Catalogues

Products

Many of the products described in this book can be found in local drug, phone and discount stores. Other devices are more medically oriented. To find them, check the yellow pages under titles such as "Home Health Products and Services," "Hospital Equipment and Supplies," and "Rehabilitation Services."

These stores will stock or have access to almost all the products listed and illustrated in this book. A "get-acquainted" visit might be a good start in understanding what may be helpful.

If you cannot locate a specific item mentioned in this book, call your local hospital and ask to speak to an occupational therapist. He or she will know which stores near you sell similar items and will have access to a variety of catalogues that carry many of the products described in this book.

Specialty catalogues

Specialty catalogues can help people who live in extremely rural areas or who otherwise find it hard to get to health product stores. Many different catalogues are available. Some familiar names include Sears and Spencer Gifts. Less well-known names include Fred Sammons, Abbey Medical, Lumex and Maddox. Also check catalogues such as the ones from The Sharper Image or Brookstone. They have novelty items that, although not designed for the purpose, can help someone experiencing physical and/or sensory changes. For best results, seek the advice and training of a professional before you order and after you receive the products.

Local, State and Regional Governmental Assistance

Area Agency on Aging (AAA)

This local administrative governmental agency is responsible for carrying out programs mandated and funded by the federal Older Americans Act. One such program is the Information and Referral Service. This is a handy service if you have questions about an elderly family member or friend and need help. Your AAA is listed under "County Government" in the phone book. You can also call the National Eldercare Locator number at (800) 677-1116 or access it on the Internet at **www.aoa.dhhs.gov**.

Many AAAs are familiar with home modification issues. Their ability to help you with products and devices varies depending on the training provided within each agency. Still, if you are new to the "aging network," this is a good place to get acquainted.

Assistive technology projects

In 1988, Congress passed the Technology-Related Assistance for Individuals with Disabilities Act. It established a clearinghouse in all states for information and funding coordination for assistive technology. These state Tech-Act programs can help you find resources in your area and answer questions you may have about funding.

The national Technical Assistance Project can direct you to the Tech-Act program in your state. Call the RESNA Technical Assistance Project at (703) 524-6686. Their fax number is (703) 524-6630, or you can reach them through the Internet at **www.resna.org**.

Regional Disability and Business Technical Assistance Center (DBTAC)

If you need information or technical help regarding the Americans with Disabilities Act (ADA), call (800) 949-4232. Your call will automatically be forwarded to your regional DBTAC. The center can provide information on how the ADA may affect you. The ADA deals with housing, transportation, communications and public access issues.

Professional Resources

Many of the following resources are organizations of members who specialize in certain professions, such as pediatrics or geriatrics. You can call these organizations for more information about their specialties. They can also help you find a practitioner who lives in your area. The "centers" listed are more concerned with product development and can provide you with product-related information.

American Association of Homes and Services for the Aging
901 E St. N.W., Suite 500
Washington, DC 20004-2011
Phone: (202) 783-2242
Fax: (202) 783-2255
www.aahsa.org

The American Occupational Therapy Association, Inc.
4720 Montgomery Lane
P.O. Box 31220
Bethesda, MD 20824
Phone: (301) 652-2682
TTY: (800) 377-8555
Fax: (301) 652-7711
www.aota.org

American Physical Therapy Association
1111 N. Fairfax St.
Alexandria, VA 22314
Phone: (703) 684-2782 or
(800) 999-APTA, ext. 3395
Fax: (703) 684-7343
www.apta.org

American Speech-Language-Hearing Association
10801 Rockville Pike
Rockville, MD 20852
Phone: (800) 638-8255
TTY: (301) 571-0457
www.asha.org

Assisted Living Federation of America
10300 Eaton Place, Suite 400
Fairfax, VA 22030
Phone: (703) 691-8100
Fax: (703) 691-8106
www.alfa.org

Center for Assistive Technology
University at Buffalo
515 Kimball Tower
3435 Main St.
Buffalo, NY 14214-3079
Phone: (716) 829-3141
TTY: (800) 628-2281
Fax: (716) 829-3217
www.wings.buffalo.edu\go?cat

Closing the Gap
P.O. Box 68
Henderson, MN 56044
Phone: (507) 248-3294
www.closingthegap.com

IBM Independent Series Information Center for People with Special Needs
Phone: (800) 426-4832
TTY: (800) 426-4833
www.ibm.com/sns

International Society for
Augmentative and Alternative
Communication (ISAAC)
49 The Donway West
Suite 308
Toronto, ON
M3C 3M9
Canada
Phone: (416) 385-0351
Fax: (416) 385-0352
E-mail: isaac_mail@mail.cepp.org
www.isaac-online.org

Iowa State University Extension
62 Le Baron Hall
Ames, IA 50011
Phone: (515) 294-8520
www.extension.iastate.edu/pages/
  housing/other/housing
  (Select "Elderly and Disabled" on
  the menu)

**National Association for
Home Care**
228 7th St. S.E.
Washington, DC 20003
Phone: (202) 547-7424
Fax: (202) 547-3540
www.nahc.org

**National Association of Professional
Geriatric Care Managers**
1604 N. Country Club Road
Tuscon, AZ 85716-3102
Phone: (520) 881-8008
Fax: (520) 325-7925
www.caremanager.org

**National Rehabilitation
Information Center (NARIC)**
1010 Wayne Ave.
Suite 800
Silver Spring, MD 20910
Phone: (800) 346-2742
TTY: (301) 495-5626
Fax: (301) 562-2401
www.naric.com

RESNA Technical Assistance Project
1700 N. Moore St.
Suite 1540
Arlington, VA 22209-1903
Phone: (703) 524-6686, ext. 313
TTY: (703) 524-6639
Fax: (703) 524-6630
www.resna.org

National Rehabilitation Association
633 S. Washington St.
Alexandria, VA 22314
Phone: (703) 836-0850
TTY: (703) 836-0849
E-mail: info@nationalrehab.org
www.nationalrehab.org

Organizations

These organizations vary in size dramatically. One may have a single office; another may have offices across the country. All of them will have print material explaining who they are and what they do. If they don't have the information you seek, ask them for other sources to contact.

AARP
Disability Initiative
601 E St. N.W.
Washington, DC 20049
Phone: (202) 434-2277 or
(800) 424-3410
TTY: (877) 434-7598
www.aarp.org

Alexander Graham Bell Association for the Deaf and Hard of Hearing
3417 Volta Place N.W.
Washington, DC 20007-2778
Phone and TTY: (202) 337-5220
Fax: (202) 337-8314
www.agbell.org

Alzheimer's Association
919 N. Michigan Ave., Suite 1100
Chicago, IL 60611
Phone: (312) 335-8700 or
(800) 272-3900
Fax: (312) 335-1110
www.alz.org

American Council of the Blind
1155 15th St. N.W.
Suite 1004
Washington, DC 20005
Phone: (800) 424-8666,
(answered from 2 to 5 p.m. EST) or
(202) 467-5081
Fax: (202) 467-5085
www.acb.org

American Speech-Language-Hearing Association
10801 Rockville Pike
Rockville, MD 20852
Phone: (800) 638-8255
TTY: (301) 571-0457
www.asha.org

The ARC (formerly the Association of Retarded Citizens)
1010 Wayne Ave.
Suite 650
Silver Spring, MD 20910
Phone: (301) 565-3842
Fax: (301) 565-3843
www.thearc.org

Arthritis Foundation
1330 W. Peachtree St.
Atlanta, GA 30309
Phone: (800) 283-7800
(automated response line) or
(404) 872-7100
www.arthritis.org

The Association of Lutheran Older Adults
Valparaiso University
Valparaiso, IN 46383
Phone: (219) 464-6743 or
(800) 930-2562
E-mail: aloa1@juno.com

Brain Injury Association
105 N. Alfred
Alexandria, VA 22314
Phone: (800) 444-6443
www.biausa.org

Council for Disability Rights
205 W. Randolph
Suite 1650
Chicago, IL 60606
Phone: (312) 444-9484
TTY: (312) 444-1967
Fax: (312) 444-1977
www.disabilityrights.org

Easter Seals
230 W. Monroe
Suite 1800
Chicago, IL 60606
Phone: (312) 726-6200
TTY: (312) 726-4258
Fax: (312) 726-1494
www.easter-seals.org

Health Resource Center for Women With Disabilities
Rehabilitation Institute of Chicago
345 E. Superior
Chicago, IL 60611
Phone: (312) 238-1051
E-mail: webmaster@rehabchicago.org
www.rehabchicago.org

HEATH Resource Center
American Council on Education
1 Dupont Circle N.W.
Suite 800
Washington, DC 20036-1193
Phone: (202) 939-9320 or
(800) 544-3284
Fax: (202) 833-5696
www.heath-resource-center.org

Lighthouse International
111 E. 59th St., 12th Floor
New York, NY 10022
Phone: (212) 821-9200 or
(800) 829-0500
Fax: (212) 821-9728
www.lighthouse.org

Muscular Dystrophy Association
3300 E. Sunrise Dr.
Tucson, AZ 85718
Phone: (520) 529-2000 or
(800) 572-1717
www.mdausa.org

National Council on Independent Living
1916 Wilson Blvd., Suite 209
Arlington, VA 22201
Phone: (703) 525-3406
TTY: (703) 525-4153
www.ncil.org

National Federation of the Blind
1800 Johnson St.
Baltimore, MD 21230
Phone: (410) 659-9314
Fax: (410) 685-5653
www.nfb.org

National Multiple Sclerosis Society
733 Third Ave.
New York, NY 10017
Phone: (800) 344-4867
www.nmss.org

National Organization on
Disability (NOD)
910 16th St. N.W., Suite 600
Washington, DC 20006
Phone: (202) 293-5960
TTY: (202) 293-5968
E-mail: ability@nod.org
www.nod.org

National Spinal Cord Injury
Association
8701 Georgia Ave.
Suite 500
Silver Spring, MD 20910
Phone: (800) 962-9629 or
(301) 588-6959
Fax: (301) 588-9414
www.spinalcord.org

National Parkinson Foundation
1501 N.W. 9th Ave.
Bob Hope Road
Miami, FL 33136-1494
Phone: (800) 327-4545 or
(305) 547-6666
www.parkinson.org

The Parkinson's Institute
1170 Morse Ave.
Sunnyvale, CA 94089-1605
Phone: (408) 734-2800 or
(800) 786-2958
www.parkinsonsinstitute.org

Self Help for Hard of Hearing
People, Inc.
7910 Woodmont Ave.
Suite 1200
Bethesda, MD 20814
Phone: (301) 657-2248
TTY: (301) 657-2249
http://shhh.org

Technical Aids and Assistance for
Persons with Disabilities
1640 W. Roosevelt Road
Chicago, IL 60608
Phone: (312) 421-3373
E-mail: taad@interaccess.com
http://homepage.interaccess.com/~taad

Trace Research &
Development Center
University of Wisconsin-Madison
5901 Research Park Blvd.
Madison, WI 53719-1252
Phone: (608) 262-6966
TTY: (608) 263-5408
http://trace.wisc.edu

United Cerebral Palsy Associations
1660 L. St. N.W.
Suite 700
Washington, DC 20036
Phone: (800) 872-5827
TTY: (202) 973-7197
www.ucpa.org

Publications

These publications range from technical resources to simple catalogs. If you can, call first to see if the publication provides the information you're looking for, and if it's written in a style that is easily understood.

Assisted Living Resource Guide—2nd Edition (1995)
Features an annotated bibliography, reference chart, inventory of pertinent organizations and institutions and a list of related journals and newsletters. $10.

Home Modifications Resource Guide—2nd Edition (1995)
Includes an annotated bibliography, reference chart, inventory of organizations, and list of related journals and agencies. $12.

National Directory of Home Modification and Repair Programs (1995)
Features an annotated directory of private/public home modification and repair programs across the country. $15.

The above publications are geared toward professionals, but include references that can be helpful to consumers. To order any of the three publications, contact:

> The National Resource Center on Supportive Housing and Home Modification
> University of Southern California
> Andrus Gerontology Center
> 3715 McClintock Ave.
> Los Angeles, CA 90089-0191
> Phone: (213) 740-1364
> www.homemods.org

Assistive Products: An Illustrated Guide to Terminology
Gordon C. Krantz, Ph.D, Margaret A. Christenson, MPH, OTR, and Adam Lindquist, B.S. ©1998/ISBN 1-56900-089-1. Available through The American Occupational Therapy Association, P.O. Box 3800, Forrester Center, WV 25438. Phone: (800) 648-7834. Fax: (800) 525-5562. $37 ($30 for AOTA members).

Home Planning for Your Later Years: New Designs, Living Options, Smart Decisions, How to Finance It.
William K. Wasch. George Dodson (Photographer), Fisher Books. ©1996/ISBN 1-886657-07-6. $19.95. Available in bookstores.

Home Safety Guide for Older People: Check It Out/Fix It Up
Jon Pynoos and Evelyn Cohen. Serif Press, Inc., 4019 5th Road N.,
Arlington, VA 22203. Prepaid orders only, $13.95 + $4.50 for shipping.
Call (703) 465-5222.

*Living in the State of Stuck: How Technology Impacts the Lives
of People with Disabilities*
M. Scherer. ISBN 0-914797-84-0 (cloth), ISBN 0-914797-81-6 (paper).
Brookline Books, P.O. Box 381047, Cambridge, MA 02238-1047. $17.95.
Call (617) 868-0360 or (800) 666-2665.

Make Your House a Home for a Lifetime: Ideas for Independent Living
The Hartford. 200 Executive Blvd., Southington, CT 06489 Attn: Hartford
House Brochure. Price: free (single copies). Includes a list of 153 products and
ideas, and 69 potential product suppliers.

*Primary Care for Persons With Disabilities: Access to
Assistive Technology: Guidelines for the Use of Assistive Technology:
Evaluation, Referral, Prescription*
Available from Clinical and Public Health Practice and Outcomes,
American Medical Association, 515 N. State St., Chicago, IL 60610. $5.
Call (312) 464-5085 or (800) 621-8335.

Resources for Elders With Disabilities
Resources for Rehabilitation, 33 Bedford St., Suite 19A, Lexington, MA 02420.
ISBN 0-929718-240. $49.95 + $5 shipping and handling. Call (781) 862-6455.
Fax: (781) 861-7517.

Safety for Older Consumers: Home Safety Checklist (Publication order #701)
U.S. Consumer Product Safety Commission Publication Request,
Washington, DC 20207. Price: free. Read this on the Internet at **www.cpsc.gov**
(select the "Library" link) or call (800) 638-2772, ext. 568.

The DoAble Renewable Home: Making Your Home Fit Your Needs
Request item D12470. AARP Fulfillment Center, 601 E St. N.W.,
Washington, DC 20091. Price: free (single copies).

The Self-Help Sourcebook
American Self-Help Clearinghouse, St. Claire's Hospital, 25 Pocono Road,
Denville, NJ 07834. $10. Call (973) 625-9565. TTY: (973) 625-9053.
Fax: (973) 625-8848.

AAL QualityLife Resources

AAL QualityLife Resources also provides other books that offer helpful information. Three examples are:

Getting the Most Out of Medicare and Medicare Supplement Insurance

This book helps readers understand their Medicare coverage and shows how to cover the gaps in times of need. It covers Medicare Part A and Part B, Medicare supplement insurance, other insurance, how to help Medicare and other insurance to be most effective, Medicare appeals, as well as helpful consumer tips for saving money.

- Gold Award winner, Mature Media National Awards Program.
- Bronze Award winner in the National Health Information Awards Program.

A Time to Mourn, A Time to Dance: Help for the Losses in Life
by Margaret Metzgar, M.A., CMHC

Here is help for anyone who wants to understand grief—grievers as well as persons who want to improve their ability to help those who are experiencing a loss.

The different faces of loss—death of a spouse, child or pet, suicide, physical loss, divorce, job loss, silent losses and positive losses—are all covered. A special section on giving help to others and holding on to hope after a loss is included. Inspiring quotes, practical tips and lists, and valuable support resources round out this compassionate guide.

Keep Kids Safe: A Parent's Guide to Child Safety

Technically reviewed by the National Safety Council and favorably reviewed by the American Academy of Family Physicians Foundation.

Accidents, especially accidents involving children, can be prevented. This comprehensive, yet easy-to-read guide shows how. It offers practical, hands-on advice to remind parents of some of the most common and easily countered threats to children. Endorsed by the National Safety Council, it features practical guidance on preventing accidents at home and away, along with a section on emergency procedures if an accident occurs.

Chapters cover: fall-related injuries, sudden infant death syndrome, fire and burns, poison, choking, motor vehicle accidents, child abduction, drowning, guns, sporting injuries, and Internet threats to children. Filled with charming cartoon illustrations, it concludes with a resource guide and Family Safety Checklist that reviews safety tools. This book belongs in the home of every family, along with a first-aid kit and emergency phone numbers.

Videos

"A Home For All Ages Sampler"
Produced by Department of Human Development and Family Studies, Iowa State University, 62 Le Baron Hall, Ames, IA 50011. $15. Call (515) 294-8520.

"Changing Needs, Changing Homes: Adapting Your Home to Fit You"
Produced by the American Occupational Therapy Association. $35.
Call toll-free (877) 404-2682 or order online at **www.aota.org** (go to "AOTA's Online Store").

"Fair Housing Means Universal Design-I"
Produced by the Center for Inclusive Design and Environmental Access, School of Architecture and Planning, University at Buffalo, Buffalo, NY 14214-3087. $35. Call (716) 829-3485, ext. 329. Fax: (716) 829-3861. E-mail address: idea@arch.buffalo.edu. This video features helpful bathroom designs. Also available is a video on kitchen designs called "Fair Housing Means Universal Design-II."

"Maintaining Seniors' Independence Through Home Adaptations"
Produced by Canada Mortgage and Housing Corporation. $22.90 for the video, shipping and other fees. To order, call (613) 748-2003 (outside of Canada) or (800) 668-2642 (in Canada) and ask for the Order Center. Fax: (613) 748-2016. Internet: **www.cmhc-schl.gc.ca**.

"Staying Home: Ways for Older Americans to Make Their Homes Fit Their Needs"
Produced by South East Senior Housing Initiative, 10 S. Wolfe St., Baltimore, MD 21231. $25. Open- or closed-captioned. Comes with companion booklet. Call (410) 327-6193. Deals with issues such as lighting, safety on stairs and conveniences. Includes interviews with seniors. Good family viewing.

"Why Move? Improve: Lifelong Comfort in Your Home"
Produced by AARP. Send request with check or money order to AARP, Consumer Issues, Housing Section, 601 E St. N.W., Washington, DC 20049. $4.50. Features interviews with people who have made modifications to their homes. Great for family viewing.

Electronic Assistive Technology Resources

Online information

The following list helps people who prefer to use computers to obtain information. America Online and CompuServe are electronic services that give you access to a wide range of resources. You must have an account with these services to access them. Others such as Trace Research & Development Center and MatureMart can provide product and service information through their Internet sites for no fee.

Alliance for Technology Access
2175 E. Francisco Blvd.
Suite L
San Rafael, CA 94901
Phone: (800) 455-7970 or
(415) 455-4575
www.ataccess.org

America Online Foundation
22000 AOL Way
Dulles, VA 20166
Phone: (703) 448-8700 or
(888) 265-8001
www.aol.com
  (Members go to keyword **disability**)

Apple Computer, Inc.
www.apple.com/education/
K12/disability

CompuServe
CompuServe Information Service
5000 Arlington Centre Blvd.
Columbus, OH 43220
Phone: (800) 336-6823
www.compuserve.com

Closing the Gap
P.O. Box 68
Henderson, MN 56044
Phone: (507) 248-3294
Fax: (507) 248-3810
www.closingthegap.com

Deaftech, USA
4 Stanley Drive
Framingham, MA 01701
Phone and TTY: (508) 620-1777
www.deaftek.org

**IBM Independent Series
Information Center**
Phone: (800) 426-4832
TTY: (800) 426-4833
www.ibm.com/sns

**National Rehabilitation Information
Center (NARIC)**
1010 Wayne Ave.
Suite 800
Silver Spring, MD 20910
Phone: (800) 346-2742
Fax: (301) 562-2401
www.naric.com

Trace Research &
Development Center
5901 Research Park Blvd.
Madison, WI 53719
Phone: (608) 262-6966
TTY: (608) 263-5408
Fax: (608) 262-8488
www.trace.wisc.edu

World Institute on Disability
510 16th St.
Suite 100
Oakland, CA 94612-1500
Phone: (510) 763-4100
TTY: (510) 208-9496
Fax: (510) 763-4109
www.wid.org

Online information and shopping

You can use the Internet to access information and purchase products. To get
you started, three Web sites are listed below. Remember, though, you may see a
product online that a local store carries for the same or a lower price. By
shopping around locally, you could save the cost of shipping and handling.
Neither AAL nor the authors of this book represent or endorse in any way
these sites or the products/services that they provide.

www.maturemart.com
An online supermarket of products similar to those that are featured in this
book. Provides a great opportunity to get information on specific products.

www.independentliving.com
Provides additional information and a "Can-Do™ Products" catalogue.

www.lib.uchicago.edu/~rd13/hd/daily.html
Provides additional information. In the listing of resources for daily living,
look for "Functional Solutions for Independent Living."

Evaluation Tools for the Home

Two basic evaluation tools are available to help find solutions to problems loved ones may experience living at home. The first is a home evaluation checklist. They're available in many forms and usually can be completed without the need of a professional. Examples can be found in such publications as the *Home Safety Guide for Older People: Check It Out/Fix It Up,* listed on page 81 in this book.

The second tool is an assessment, which should be done by an occupational therapist or other appropriate professional. This assessment not only evaluates what an older person cannot do, but more importantly, what he or she can do. To locate an occupational therapist, call your local hospital or contact The American Occupational Therapy Association at the address or phone number listed on page 75.

Using both of these evaluation tools can help a person live independently with the fewest problems.

Other Housing Options for Older Adults

Sometimes it becomes impractical for a person to remain in his or her home because of failing health, loneliness, inability to maintain the upkeep of a home, lack of transportation, or the distance of home from stores, activities, and services. When living at home is no longer feasible or desirable, one option to consider is senior housing. People frequently find that a move into senior housing results in their needs being better met; less isolation; increased involvement in social and recreational activities; and a greater feeling of security, independence, and freedom.

However, with any group living, there are disadvantages. There can be a degree of regimentation and some loss of privacy. Such changes may be difficult for people who do not like to eat on a schedule and prefer their own space. To help ensure a successful relocation, look for a place that provides for people's privacy, while unobtrusively monitoring their situation.

A variety of housing options are available to meet the varied needs of older people. These include:

Retirement communities

Retirement communities are for active retired people. Housing types and sizes vary greatly. They include single family dwellings, townhouses, duplexes, highrise apartments, condominiums, and mobile homes. Living units may be for rent or sale.

Retirement communities may or may not provide support services. In many communities, only the usual community services such as police and fire protection are provided. Others provide recreational and social activities, household maintenance and repair. Some retirement complexes offer a range of services—housekeeping, group dining, transportation for special events, shopping and medical appointments—for an additional fee. A few have infirmaries for short-term nursing care; long-term nursing care usually is not available.

Applicants generally must be independent in all activities of daily living (able to bathe, dress and take medication without assistance), mentally alert, have bowel and bladder control, and be able to walk. Some facilities allow walkers and wheelchairs.

Continuing care retirement communities (CCRCs)

A continuing care retirement community (also called "life care") offers lifetime housing. It includes independent living, personal care and nursing services. It can be a way to assure independent but supportive living, as long as possible in the same setting. This provides a guarantee that nursing care is available if needed. Residents may move from one care level to another as their needs change. Multiple levels of support can be particularly advantageous to couples, enabling both to stay in the same community, even when one partner needs nursing home care. Another advantage is that a support system can remain uninterrupted as needs change.

Continuing care retirement communities usually offer a variety of services. These may include personal conveniences (beauty and barbershops, banks, library); organized social and recreational activities; educational programs; exercise classes; craft and woodworking room; gardening space; transportation; and health care.

Some CCRCs provide full health care benefits at no additional charge. Others offer full care with additional charges, after a specific number of days of health care per year. Still others charge for certain medical services. Because of the many services and activities available, living in a continuing care retirement community can be costly. There is usually a substantial entrance fee plus monthly charges.

Because of the financial investment required in a CCRC, a person should visit several times before making a commitment. If guest quarters are available, it may be wise to stay in the community a few nights to get a better feel for the surroundings, activities, residents and staff.

Admission requirements are generally restrictive regarding minimum age, health and finances.

Congregate housing

Congregate housing (sometimes called "assisted independent living") is for the person who needs little or no assistance. Residents have their own private apartments, including a kitchenette for light meals and snacks. Basic hotel-type services are provided, for example daily meals, light housekeeping, non-personal laundry, organized social and recreational activities, transportation and security services. Some services may be optional. Many have emergency signaling devices in bedrooms and bathrooms for summoning help.

Most require residents to be able to live independently. Cost varies depending on the housing and services provided.

Low-income housing

In recent years, many communities have built housing for older people with low and moderate incomes. Rents are subsidized and, therefore, lower than market rents. Rent is adjusted to a percentage of a resident's income.

In some areas, a short supply of units requires a person to be on a waiting list for several months. For information about low-income housing, contact the local housing authority.

Residential care facility

A residential care facility (sometimes called "board and care home," "personal care," "sheltered housing" or "domiciliary care home") may be the answer for a person who needs some supervision or assistance with personal care. Some facilities have studio or one-bedroom units. Typically, they lack kitchenettes but have private bathrooms. Other facilities have private or shared rooms. Sharing a room can be a difficult adjustment for some people.

Residential care facilities are generally licensed (but not in all states) and must meet design and operating standards, including minimum staff requirements. Staff coverage is provided 24 hours a day. Prospective residents generally must be mentally alert; able to dress, feed and take themselves to the toilet; and able to eat meals in a central dining room.

Assisted living facility

Assisted living facilities are a specific type of residential care facility. They generally feature apartments, often with kitchenettes. Services vary but are generally similar to those offered by residential care facilities.

Regulations and licensing requirements vary from state to state, contributing to a wide range of facilities that are called assisted living. In some states, financial help may be available through medical assistance programs. However, many assisted living facilities accept only private-pay residents.

Adult foster care

Adult foster care (also called "adult family homes") is provided in a private home occupied by an individual or family. Care can range from simple room and board with laundry and transportation provided, to help with bathing, dressing, toileting and feeding. The level of care given depends on the provider's background, training and interests.

A potential resident is typically a person who is mentally alert to moderately confused, needs some assistance with personal care and/or 24-hour supervision. Usually, the person must have bowel and bladder control and be able to walk or use a cane, walker or wheelchair. Foster care providers generally will not accept persons who wander because they cannot leave other residents to search for the wanderer.

Nursing home

A nursing home is an extended care facility that can offer a range of services, including skilled, intermediate and rehabilitative care. If a person is seriously ill and needs extensive or continuous nursing care or 24-hour supervision, a nursing home may be the best choice.

In some states, preadmission screening is available, or required, for admission. A team of professionals assess the older person's functioning, the type of care needed, the appropriateness of placement and possible alternatives. (Some states also require preadmission screening for other types of care facilities.)

Nursing homes provide three levels of care: custodial, intermediate and skilled.

- Custodial care: For people who primarily require supervision and help with personal care and other activities of daily living.
- Intermediate care: For people who need supervision and assistance with personal care and some medical attention, but not round-the-clock nursing care. Intermediate care also may be appropriate for people who need certain rehabilitation services. Care is ordered by a physician and supervised by a registered or licensed nurse.
- Skilled nursing care: For people who need 24-hour medical supervision, skilled nursing care or rehabilitation, but do not need hospitalization. This

care might be appropriate for a person recovering from a broken hip, recent stroke or an illness that requires round-the-clock nursing care. Care is provided by a registered nurse under the direction of a doctor. A physician's order is required for admission. Medicare may pay for skilled nursing care, under specific conditions or provisions.

Some facilities also have special care units that are specifically designed to meet the needs of people who have Alzheimer's disease or other dementia.

Housing choices

The names of various housing/care arrangements are not universal. Different words may be used in different communities, regions or states. The Area Agency on Aging and local housing authority are good resources to contact when investigating housing options. Also, look in the yellow pages of your telephone directory under Retirement Homes and Nursing Homes. For information about religiously affiliated homes, call a local church of the particular faith or denomination.

The best housing choice depends on a person's needs, level of functioning and financial resources. These needs may change with time, requiring a person to consider another option. Therefore, it's wise to consider housing possibilities before changes arise. The goal is to select housing that offers the greatest degree of personal independence, while meeting safety, comfort and convenience needs. Generally, the more extensive the services, the more costly the housing.

About the Authors

Information for this booklet was provided by Dennis R. La Buda, M.A., and Vicki Schmall, Ph.D.

Dennis R. La Buda, M.A.

A gerontological consultant in private practice, La Buda is president of Tech-AGE Resources, San Francisco, California, and Olympia, Washington. His expertise relates to the impact of technological and environmental development on our aging population. He is recognized for a broad range of contributions to the field of gerontology. La Buda edited *The Gadget Book,* a product resource guide published for the American Society on Aging featuring devices designed to make everyday living easier.

Vicki Schmall, Ph.D.

Schmall is a gerontology and training specialist and president of Aging Concerns in West Linn, Oregon. She is known for developing many educational programs and resources on various aspects of aging for professionals, practitioners and families. She is a professor emeritus of gerontology at Oregon State University.

Special thanks to Anne Long-Morris, Ph.D., former geriatric program manager for the American Occupational Therapy Association. Morris now has a private practice, Elder Care Solutions, in Springfield, Virginia. Also, thanks to Joan Rogers, Ph.D., professor of occupational therapy, School of Health and Rehabilitation Sciences, University of Pittsburgh.

Illustrations

Illustrations in this publication, whether reproduced or rendered from *The Gadget Book,* appear courtesy of Dennis R. LaBuda. They do not represent any specific product, nor do they imply any form of endorsement.